THE RED REVOLUTION

THE RED REVOLUTION

Liverpool Under Houllier

Conrad Mewton

MAINSTREAM
PUBLISHING

EDINBURGH AND LONDON

To Katharina for all her help and support and to
Paul Tomkins for the original inspiration.

First published in Great Britain in 2002 by
MAINSTREAM PUBLISHING (EDINBURGH) LTD
7 Albany Street
Edinburgh EH1 3UG

ISBN 1 84018 627 5

A catalogue record for this book is available from the British Library

Typeset in Garamond and Gill

Printed in Great Britain by
Mackays of Chatham PLC

Contents

Introduction

The Spice Boys

Out they strode, seemingly unaware of the mirth-inducing nature of their outfits, the 'cream' of Liverpool's footballers, resplendent in all-white Giorgio Armani suits that wouldn't have looked out of place propping up the bar at the Copacabana, to sample the atmosphere of Wembley Stadium. Oh yes, a football match was about to take place – not just any football match, but the 1996 FA Cup final between those old adversaries, Manchester United and Liverpool, before a worldwide audience of many millions. And Liverpool had arrived for the big occasion dressed, as Robbie Fowler later described it, 'like ice cream salesmen'.

In the days when the traditions of the FA Cup still counted for something (before it became the norm to play third-round ties before January, or field your reserve side, or swan off to Brazil and give the tournament a miss altogether), Liverpool's appearance on Wembley's hallowed turf in their ill-judged pre-match attire was an affront to the dignity of the occasion. And it was also bloody funny, at least if you weren't a fan of the club. It wouldn't have been such a public relations disaster if the team had gone on to win the match, or at least performed to a level worthy of the showpiece event. The final, however, singularly failed to live up to expectations. Liverpool's performance was as chequered as their unrecognisable change strip, as dismal as their pre-match suits had been bright. Neither side, in fact, were able to produce the flowing football upon which they had built their reputations over the course of the season. The game was ultimately decided when, with extra time beckoning, Eric Cantona drove home a half-volley from the edge of a crowded penalty area, after a corner had been only partially cleared – a fine goal out of keeping with a scrappy match. A defeat for Liverpool, but more significantly, a dark day in the club's history: the day when the whole world found out how far the rot had set in at a once-great club.

When, three months after the Wembley fiasco, the new football season was heralded by the Spice Girls' 'Wannabe' spending its umpteenth week at number one in the charts, the sometime catwalk models, sometime footballers from the red half of Merseyside had a new nickname befitting their status as virtual pop stars: 'the Spice Boys'. And much as they publicly claimed to despise such a tag, the off-field shenanigans and on-field performances of David James, Steve McManaman, Jamie Redknapp, Robbie Fowler, Stan Collymore, Neil Ruddock and Jason 'try this shampoo and conditioner' McAteer did little to diminish its use in the coming months.

Not that the 'Spice Boys' tag was necessarily all bad, redolent as it was of sexy, exciting football (though, alas, not the kind of football that is too attentive to dull, menial tasks like tackling back and defending). Although Liverpool ultimately failed to mount a credible bid for the title in either of the seasons that followed that Cup final defeat to Manchester United, some of the football they played during that period was sublime. Going forward, they remained the most exhilarating team in the Premiership, as McManaman, a mop-haired blur of shimmies and feints, tore at defences from all angles, Fowler, the magician of the penalty area, conjured up all manner of finishes, from the exquisite to the venomous and the Reds' new Czech import, Patrik Berger, dealt exclusively, it seemed, in left-footed drives arrowed into the corner of the goal from long distance – each celebrated with a right arm joyously punching the sky (and a quick adjustment of the Alice band).

But Liverpool's attacking, flowing football brought no trophies.

Failure to land the Premiership title in 1996–97 was particularly galling because Liverpool for so long looked capable of matching United stride for stride. When the pressure was on, however, the team fell away badly, losing to lowly Coventry and Wimbledon during the run-in. More critically, they were emphatically beaten (3–1) at Anfield by eventual champions Manchester United. United's first two goals, like both of Coventry's in their shock 2–1 win in Liverpool's previous home match, were headers scored directly from corners (United's third was also a header after James flapped at – and missed – a cross). It seemed as though every time their opponents won a corner, they regarded it as almost akin to a penalty kick. Liverpool's inability to defend set-pieces, and their defensive frailties generally, hurt them time and again under manager Roy Evans. Their confidence dented by another defeat to their bitterest rivals, Liverpool could only muster a fourth-place finish.

The following year, many observers felt Evans simply had to win the championship if he was to keep his job. But 1997–98 was, if anything, a step back from the previous season. Liverpool finished some distance behind Arsenal and Manchester United, defeats to the league's makeweights – Derby, Leicester, Barnsley and West Ham – costing them dear. Worse still, the Reds seemed no nearer to regaining what they saw as their rightful place in Europe. Both the 1996–97 and 1997–98 campaigns were notable for shambolic defensive performances that were an embarrassment to the club's rich heritage. Heavy defeats to Paris St Germain and Strasbourg, following on from a home reverse to Danish part-timers Brondby in 1995–96, confirmed what the rest of Europe had suspected for some time: Liverpool were no longer a football superpower. They were trading on past glories for their continued place as a member of Europe's elite G14 clubs.

Success on the field would, of course, have deflected, probably even eradicated, any meaningful criticism of the players' off-field activities. Without it, there was nowhere to hide. The 1996 Cup final was perhaps the most public example, but the dilettante image the Spice Boys tag evoked – of a life of unremitting glamour spent in exclusive wine bars, driving Ferraris and BMWs, attending film premieres, modelling Boss and Versace suits – was anathema to those fans of the club brought up on an unwavering diet of hard-earned success under a succession of dour Scotsmen, from Shankly and Paisley through to Dalglish (we'll pass over Souness). In their headier moments, Liverpool's stars seemed to be living by the maxim of original Spice Boy George Best ('I spend most of my money on booze, birds and fast cars. The rest I just squander'), without achieving the results to match: the *Loaded* lager culture of the mid-'90s was a prevailing influence on the Spice Boy clique of the Liverpool squad, where a well-known catchphrase among the players was 'Win or lose – hit the booze'. Unfortunately, booze all too often followed lose.

But football had moved on from George Best's day. It was unrecognisable, in fact, from only ten years before. Liverpool's all-conquering 1984 side prepared for the European Cup final against Roma by famously going on a drinking holiday in Spain to relax and unwind after the demands of a difficult season. They went on to win the game on penalties, having matched their opponents through 120 minutes of what, viewed today, appears as footage from an altogether different era. The build-up play was patient, the pace measured; both sides made ample use of the back-pass to the goalkeeper. Changes in the game's laws after the dreary Italia '90 World Cup, where many of the knock-out ties were decided on penalties with the score 0–0 or 1–1 after extra time (in particular, preventing the goalkeeper from picking up back-passes, and altering the offside rule to favour the attacking side) served to quicken the pace of the game. When combined with the huge strides being made in player fitness and diet, football became fast and furious, 90 minutes of unrelenting action. It made for a more exciting spectacle, but the physical demands on the top players was intense. Liverpool's players under Roy Evans (many internationals, competing all year round) did not seem capable of maintaining the consistent mental and physical application an exhausting Premier League season required.

After nearly a decade during which Liverpool had won only two trophies and had failed to impose themselves either in the championship or in Europe (the twin bases upon which they earned their reputation), something had to give. Perhaps the methods and habits that had got the club into such a pre-eminent position were no longer as effective as they should be. Difficult though it was to accept, the Liverpool hierarchy, driven by Chairman David Moores and Executive Vice-Chairman Peter Robinson, realised the club would have to embrace change if they were to compete with Manchester United, Arsenal and Europe's premier sides. The Boot Room tradition of always grooming and then appointing a new manager from within had reached the end of the line. It was time to seek outside help, to re-evaluate every element of the club's structure from the grassroots up: the methods of the coaching staff, the dietary habits of the players, transfer policy, youth development and team tactics, the wage structure, and the commercial and marketing arm. A new discipline had to be instilled across every tier of the club if Liverpool was to rid itself of its unwanted image as European football's sleeping giant.

Throughout the 1997–98 season, as it became clearer week by week that Evans had taken the team as far as he could, Moores and Robinson put everything they could into finding the right man for the task, their mission summed up by Moores' statement of intent: 'It's a massive, massive club, the most successful club in England, and we want to get it back to that state.' After nine months and another trophy-less season of underachievement, the summer of 1998 arrived with a schoolmasterly but passionate Frenchman ready and willing to be installed at Anfield. In Gérard Houllier, a man whose football philosophy embraced the belief that 'you must compete, you must run and fight until you have nothing left', Liverpool believed they had finally found the man to turn their fortunes around. Like the prancing, pouting bunch who inspired their nickname, the Spice Boys' days were numbered.

1

Stand Up Gérard Houllier

'In football you have to prepare for success. You can't programme it.'

Gérard Houllier

May 1998. The World Cup was just about to kick off in France and a native Frenchman was in the throes of arranging the next step in a successful and varied coaching career that would take him outside his homeland for the first time. The current technical director of the French Football Federation had laid the foundations for success on the international stage; his team were now embarking on their quest to become world champions in the more than capable hands of coach Aimé Jacquet. Gérard Houllier, meanwhile, was destined for a return to day-to-day management at club level – with Scottish Premier League side Celtic.

The telephone rang and Gérard was delighted to hear the voice of the Liverpool Executive Vice-Chairman, Peter Robinson, on the other end of the line, calling to congratulate him on his new appointment. But Peter Robinson had an ulterior motive for making that fateful phone call. He was, he later admitted, 'fishing for information' to see how committed Houllier was to joining Celtic. Gérard explained that he was still negotiating the terms of his contract. Sensing his opportunity, Robinson suddenly suggested that any club Houllier joined would be the wrong one – unless it was Liverpool. Surprised but enticed by the prospect, Houllier made it clear that he was open to a formal Liverpool approach. Robinson's boldness was about to pay off.

The board of Liverpool FC quickly convened. The traditionalists were nervous and presented a case for staying with a Liverpool man. John Toshack's name was put forward, but they were talked out of what would have been a regressive appointment by Robinson, who eventually convinced them that Houllier represented Liverpool's future. An insistent Robinson may have been going out on a limb but not as far as Houllier, who met a four-man delegation headed by David Moores in Paris before taking a deep breath and opting for a challenge that he had long believed would be his destiny. Peter Robinson had known Gérard Houllier long enough to know that Gérard would not resist Liverpool's call: their friendship dated back nearly three decades to the time when, as a young French teacher, Houllier first found himself in Liverpool.

Although born in Thérouanne, France, Houllier had a long history of supporting the Reds, following their early exploits in Europe under Shankly as a teenager. The romance was consummated in September 1969 when Liverpool played Dundalk in the Fairs Cup. The youthful Houllier stood, for the first time, on the Spion Kop and watched the Reds destroy their hapless opponents 10–0. The game left an indelible impression on Houllier: 'It seems funny. The score was 5–0 at half-time but the team kept attacking until the end of the game – the Liverpool team just kept going forward! That would have been absolutely impossible in France. After four or five goals, the game would have been over. I was very impressed by that.' (Not that Houllier seemed overly inclined to follow that philosophy when he later took over the reins at Liverpool.)

Houllier's first visit to Anfield had come while he was in Merseyside on a 12-month secondment, teaching French to the 15 year olds of Form 4B at a Liverpool comprehensive and determined to forge lasting links with the club that had always entranced him. Gérard quickly became aware of the city's passion for football, recalling 'the first question I was asked was not "which part of France are you from?" but "are you red or blue?"' The young French football scholar visited Liverpool's training complex at Melwood, introduced himself to Peter Robinson and, after some persuading, was allowed to study the then manager Bill Shankly's training methods, thereby setting in motion a friendship with Liverpool's Vice Chairman that, over 25 years later, would play a significant role in Houllier's return to Melwood as manager of the club.

Now, as Houllier and Moores sat in a Paris hotel discussing the finer points of Houllier's new role as joint team manager, to work alongside Roy Evans, the wheel had turned full circle. Houllier, who had achieved so much in football in those intervening 25-plus years, could scarcely believe that he was on the threshold of realising a long-held dream: 'I can still vividly remember standing on the Kop while I was teaching on Merseyside and saying to myself that one day I would come back and manage Liverpool. It was a daydream, of course. When you consider I was in my early 20s and no one knew me, it was almost a fairytale. Watching those great players of the '70s and mingling with fans whose passion and knowledge just swept you along made a lasting impression. I always wanted to be a top coach, and I could think of nowhere better than Anfield to fulfil my dream.'

The formalities completed, Gérard Houllier was officially unveiled as Liverpool's new co-manager to more raised eyebrows than at a Roger Moore convention. Peter Robinson heralded the appointment as 'a bold and creative move'. Houllier quickly impressed his footballing philosophy on his new club, explaining: 'The reason Liverpool asked me to come was because aspects of their preparation needed changing. When the game changes, as football has in the last few years, your preparation has to change, too. In football you are never sure to succeed, but I am absolutely convinced you will fail if you do not do the right things.' Houllier faced a huge challenge in trying to recapture the glory days at Liverpool. But while he had never played football at professional level, he arrived equipped for the task. As technical director of the French Football Federation, his influence on French football had been immense, providing a fast track into the national team for outstanding youngsters and creating a model that became the envy of Europe. As part of his role, Houllier played an instrumental part in underwriting French World Cup success during the summer of 1998, receiving a special medal as recognition of his part in the triumph. Aimé Jacquet later declared: 'We owe our victory in the 1998 World Cup final to him.'

Houllier had previously been head coach of the French national side during 1992 and 1993, although with famously unfortunate results – France contrived to lose to a last-minute goal against Bulgaria to miss out on the World Cup of 1994 (David Ginola's mistake in conceding possession for Bulgaria's winner led Houllier to condemn Ginola as 'criminal'). Houllier had not found being in charge of the national side easy. 'It's a very frustrating job. It's like sleeping with the most beautiful girl in the country once a month. What do you do the rest of the time? It is better to sleep with the most beautiful girl in the town on a regular basis.'

As a manager at club level, however, Gérard Houllier had enjoyed a run of almost unbroken success. Beginning his managerial career in 1973 as player-coach at Le Touquet near Boulogne at the age of 26, Houllier progressed swiftly. He moved on to Noeux-les-Mines, at the time a provincial Third Division side with little prospect of achieving better things, as head coach in 1976. By now dubbed 'the Professor' by his players, Houllier transformed their fortunes, guiding the club to two consecutive promotions. 'He already loved English football, and Liverpool in particular,' recalled Noeux-les-Mines President of the time, Gérard Dhesse. RC Lens recruited him at the beginning of the '80s and Houllier continued on his upward spiral, winning honours and admirers in equal measure as he gradually acquired a reputation for progressive thinking, tactical acumen and perceptive analysis of the opposition. Those players who had been sceptical at first because he had not been a professional footballer were quickly won over. With Lens, Houllier achieved another promotion (to the French First Division) and, the following year, UEFA Cup qualification.

While at Lens, Gérard Houllier found time to visit his spiritual home once again. He took his assistant, Joachim Marx, with him to a classic night of European Cup football at Anfield. Marx recalled Houllier's excitement at returning to Liverpool: 'I could see from the start that something was getting to Gérard. It was the noise, the passion, the red-brick stadium, the little working-class houses all around. Gérard was spellbound by the whole thing.

'We went to a pub nearby after the game and drank a few beers. No one, of course, knew who Gérard was. He talked football with the fans just like he was one of them. As we left the pub, Gérard made a remark to me that I have never forgotten. He said: "You know, Joachim, I would love to be the coach of this club one day." I honestly believe Gérard never lost that dream.'

Leaving Lens, Houllier took another step nearer fulfilling that ambition by landing the biggest job in French club football – manager of the capital's premier side, Paris St Germain. The French Football Federation took note when Houllier won the title with PSG in 1986 in only his second season in charge. He was quickly assimilated into the national coaching set-up and given the ultimate responsibility for coaching at all levels of French football. As part of his new role within the Federation, Houllier was groomed to take over the national side and, in preparation, was appointed assistant to the French national team manager, Michel Platini. Between 1988 and 1992, Houllier worked closely with Platini, honing his coaching skills under the wing of France's greatest footballer, although the notoriously arrogant Platini remained suspicious of Houllier's failure to have played professionally to even a lower league standard, let alone at his own exalted level. At times this made for a difficult relationship between the two, although Houllier learnt much about coaching at the highest level from Platini, in particular the importance of even the most minor aspect in match preparation. He recalled: 'Michel believed that football at the top level was about detail, even the position of the players' feet at set-pieces.' Unfortunately, those lessons were unable to help Houllier avoid his first real set-back as a manager – failing to take the national team on from Platini.

After the trauma of the last gasp failure to qualify for the 1994 World Cup, Houllier resigned as manager of Les Bleus after just 12 games – and four defeats. He retreated from the spotlight into a second stint as the Federation's technical director, helping to develop further the French Football Academy at Clairefontaine and coaching the French team to success in the 1996 European Under-18 Championship, in the process working with young players of the calibre of Thierry Henry, David Trézéguet and Nicolas Anelka. (Houllier described the latter as 'Extraordinary. The most promising player of his age I have ever seen.')

Needing a new challenge and a return to the tensions and demands of club management, Houllier decided to seek a coaching position abroad. His destination was by no means inevitable, and although he looked to Britain, as an avid admirer of British football's passion and aggression, his initial contact was with Sheffield Wednesday. When the possibility of a move to Hillsborough fell through, Houllier found himself courted by Celtic and came perilously close to joining the Glasgow giants until Peter Robinson's timely intervention and, with it, the opportunity to finally realise his long-held dream.

On his arrival on Merseyside in July 1998, Gérard made a point of living in the city itself, rather than joining many of the players on the outskirts or in Southport, because he wanted to hear what Liverpool fans were saying and sense what they were feeling about the club at close quarters. Houllier was ready for the challenge of resurrecting Liverpool's fortunes. 'I remember getting to Anfield and finding I was staring at a blank page but that was all right. I needed to focus on a new objective.'

Houllier's mission in the short term was to work in tandem with the present incumbent, Roy Evans, in aiming to improve on the defensive shortcomings that had cost Liverpool a realistic shot at the title in the past few years. The side had finished third in Evans' final season in sole charge, but with only 65 points and having conceded 42 goals. On and off the pitch they were still some way behind Arsenal and Manchester United, both of whom were regularly involved in Europe's premier competition – the newly created Champions League – and were attracting high-quality players from across the continent. The Liverpool board had been particularly impressed by Arsène Wenger's transformation of an ageing, one-paced Arsenal team at Highbury and by his ability to unearth gems at knock-down prices. His plucking of Patrick Vieira from AC Milan's reserves and subsequent pairing with Emmanuel Petit made Liverpool's own recent high-profile midfield signing of the 30-year-old Paul Ince from Inter look a pedestrian, short-sighted move in comparison. Robinson and Moores knew that with Houllier they were acquiring a coach with an encyclopaedic knowledge of players across Europe and a scouting network and top-level contacts to match.

Standards had fallen so far at Anfield that, realistically, Liverpool were now playing catch-up with Arsenal and Manchester United, while looking nervously over their shoulder at the revival in fortunes gathering pace under Gullit and Vialli at Chelsea. The new dietary and disciplinary regimes instilled by Wenger and Gullit at Highbury and Stamford Bridge, together with training methods polished at Europe's top clubs, were already threatening to push the London sides further ahead of traditional, family-run Liverpool. Of all the clubs outside London, only Manchester United, as a massive plc with huge worldwide support and a stable management set-up, looked able to compete with the ability of London's biggest clubs to attract the top European footballing and coaching talent. Liverpool would have to move fast. Houllier was under no illusion of the task facing him, although he was painfully aware that a lot of people at the club were in for a shock, not least some of his players.

Houllier was adamant that footballers can only be successful through hard work and fitness, explaining that a player 'needs to be a winner every day in training. Every function, every exercise, he should be striving to win.' Soon Houllier was conducting three training sessions a day and imposing a ban on mobile phones at Melwood (a ban not always adhered to by the boss!), together with an embargo on after-match drinking sessions. While he could forgive mistakes, Houllier demanded from his squad, above all else, passion and a willingness to die for the red shirt. The ethic that underpinned his philosophy of management was talent, work and spirit. 'I won't let anybody raise a finger against the togetherness of the team otherwise I chop it immediately. The moment your club goes through a difficult period is the moment to show whether you really care for the red shirt. In the end, it is the players who must assume the responsibility. It is the players who must say "OK this is my life, my reputation on the line, and I have to do something about it."'

Typical of Houllier's unremitting desire to impose discipline on his players, and an early warning that anything less than total commitment would not be tolerated, was his decision to drop Jamie Carragher for showing a poor attitude in a reserve game. Carragher was forced to train with the youth team. Houllier explained: 'I didn't like his performance in the reserve team. It was not up to his normal standard and so I left him out of the squad to travel to Sunderland. Did he accept my judgment? Well, he had no choice. Players know what kind of performance they have put in and they know that they must be on top of their game, otherwise they won't play.'

Excessive alcohol intake was off-limits for his players. Houllier was shocked by the extent to which a drinking culture was imbued in the English game: 'In France if you tell the players they can have a drink, they have two drinks. Here they have a double figure of drinks. An individual is like a top motor-racing car. If you don't have the right liquid as well as the right food, it's just like a car if you put the wrong petrol in it. Professional football has changed. If you are not focused, if you don't devote all your time, your energy, even your diet, then you don't succeed.'

Gérard Houllier was a single-minded individual, determined and focused, with a passion for Liverpool FC and its history and tradition that had helped take him from the most unlikely of origins to manager of one of Europe's most famous clubs. He was a driven man who hardly ever slept. He once explained to his assistant at Lens (Joachim Marx) that he had picked up the habit of going without sleep as a student reading all night. Marx remembered the obsessive Houllier's many visits to his home to discuss football: 'It was funny, he would drop into my house for a chat, sit on the settee and say, "Give me five minutes." Then he would immediately fall asleep. His eyes would open five minutes later and we would start talking football.' Houllier would frequently drive Marx's wife mad by ringing up to discuss the next game's team selection and tactics in the middle of the night.

Many years later, lying in a hospital bed in the Cardiothoracic Centre at Liverpool's Broadgreen Hospital, only days after coming out of a coma following a life-threatening operation, the irascible Houllier wanted to talk football with the first journalist to be allowed access to his bedside, enthusing about Danny Murphy winning his first cap for England and delighting in the team's success in his absence. Houllier joked about befriending one of the nurses assigned to look after him and persuading him to bring a television into the ward, so Houllier could follow his team's exploits from his bed. Houllier recalled that while watching Liverpool's Champions League game in Boavista, the picture had momentarily disappeared. Shortly after, a doctor told him he wanted to take his blood pressure: 'I did not know why. The ITV picture had gone off for two minutes. That was when Danny Murphy scored. We all laughed about it. My blood pressure could have gone up with the excitement of seeing Danny's shot hit the back of the net!' There was no reining in his love of football, even in his darkest moments. Houllier explained simply, as though it were the most natural thing in the world, 'football is my oxygen, my life. That is why I was watching games even when I was in the recovery unit.'

By the onset of Gérard Houllier's health problems in the latter half of 2001, the Frenchman's status as Liverpool's most successful manager since Dalglish and most popular since Shankly was already ensured after a stunning haul of five trophies in a little over six months and a visible transformation in the attitude and discipline of his players. But it was during Houllier's five-month exile from Anfield, following his life-saving operation of 13 October, that his reputation as Liverpool's most charismatic manager since Shankly grew almost by the day. An aura of mystique now surrounded Houllier. Rumours of his movement were legion: he was recuperating with his brother, Serge, in Corsica; living in an apartment in Paris; scouting players in Auxerre; tying up a deal with Paris St Germain forward Nicolas Anelka; back on Merseyside; checking on training facilities ahead of a Champions League game in Galatasaray. Towards the latter stages of his recovery, when he *was* back in Liverpool, he broke cover to deliver a Churchillian rallying call to his players before key matches against Leeds and Newcastle. Famously, he gave a passionate and emotional speech to the board members at Liverpool's December AGM, fuelling further his image as a leader of messianic status. In his absence, Liverpool's supporters religiously chanted his name at every match, while their team's mid-season dip in form left the fans clamouring for his return. When two of Houllier's protégés, Emile Heskey and Danny Murphy, were going through a difficult time and coming in for increasing criticism from fans, Houllier spoke to both, offering an avuncular arm of support and reiterating his total faith in their ability. Their manager's pep talks proved inspirational, as both quickly repaid his confidence with match-winning displays and vastly improved form that contributed hugely to Liverpool's impressive winning streak of seven consecutive victories achieved in the final stretch of the season as they pushed Arsenal for the title.

Perhaps Houllier's masterstroke was the timing of his return to the dugout on the occasion of Liverpool's critical Champions League tie against Roma in March 2002. The decision to return to Anfield for the first time since the events of 13 October was made spontaneously after a team talk delivered earlier in the day but, while the players knew of his impending appearance, the galvanising effect of his unexpected presence on the touchline just seconds before kick-off was immeasurable. The team, already geed up, cut loose to a backdrop of incessant noise from the supporters, reaching a crescendo as Gérard stepped from the bench to deliver instructions from the technical area.

Throughout his exile Houllier had monitored his team's form closely, gradually increasing his input into tactics and selection and planning future possible signings as his health improved. He remained determined to return to his position as Liverpool's number one (from as early as mid-November, visiting Melwood to reassure his players that he would come back as manager) and unshakeable in his conviction that such a day would arrive before the 2001–02 season had reached its climax. Gérard scoffed at suggestions that he might have to retire from the game: 'Will football ever get out of my life? I tell you straight away. No! My wife knows that. So does my family. My whole life is about football.' Nonetheless, he accepted that he would need to streamline his role, perhaps relinquishing some of the more peripheral aspects of his workload, such as his position with UEFA's technical committee. He understood, too, that he needed to pace himself from now on and would have to cut back on scouting players and opponents, focusing his energies instead on the core aspects of his job in which he excelled: man-management, strategy, vision and the training and development of his players (for the first time in years, Houllier did not attend the World Cup, reluctantly accepting that he would have to follow football's greatest trade fair on television).

These qualities, together with an obsessive drive and vast footballing knowledge, made him uniquely placed, from the day he first arrived on Merseyside, to instigate the revolution or, in his own words, the 're-education' (he dislikes the word 'revolution' with all its French connotations) he knew was needed to resurrect Liverpool as the 'bastion of invincibility' first envisaged – and attained – by Shankly, and perpetuated through successive eras until the break-up of the side in the late '80s.

He just had the small matter of the debris of years of indolence to clear up first, and he had to begin his task by sharing (and perhaps fatally compromising) his vision with a co-manager weighed down by the baggage of 30 years of Boot Room rule. As fate would have it, Gérard Houllier would not have long to wait before assuming the sole responsibility for Liverpool's destiny that he craved.

2

Guillotine: Out with the Old Guard (1998–99 Season)

The 1998–99 season was a momentous ten months in the history of Liverpool FC, a litany of on- and off-field controversies and contract wrangles. The team, thanks largely to unmitigated managerial chaos in the first part of the season and Robbie Fowler's increasingly errant behaviour in the second, were rarely out of the media spotlight. 1998–99 will forever go down as the year Liverpool began their quest for the Premiership title with joint managers at the helm and ended it languishing in mid-table under the sole care of the first foreign manager to be appointed at Anfield in the club's 106-year history.

And it all began so brightly.

The nation had barely awoken from its summer slumbers as Michael Owen, a precociously talented 18 year old, already immortalised in World Cup legend for *that* goal against Argentina, fired Liverpool to an opening-day victory at Southampton. A fortnight later Ruud Gullit looked on in disbelief as his first day at St James's Park turned into a painful lesson in 'sexy football' that Newcastle's season never fully recovered from. By half-time Liverpool were 4–0 up and the Boy Wonder was playing out of his skin. A breathless hat trick and a stunning drive by Patrik Berger had even the home fans purring in appreciation. One image summed it up: after a slaloming run past three home defenders and an exquisite angled finish, Owen stood on the touchline gleefully rubbing his hands together in anticipation of a bumper harvest of goals and a season of glory. Scoring goals had never been made to look as easy as this nerveless teenager managed to make it appear that sunny Sunday afternoon.

Liverpool's home season got underway with a goalless draw against Arsenal. Players from both clubs – each heavily represented in the summer's World Cup – appeared tired. Houllier admitted that he had been taken by surprise by the speed of the English game. 'I was discussing with Arsène [Wenger] before the game that what struck me most here was the pace and tempo of the game. At times it is practically impossible to put your foot on the ball and see what you are doing. In continental football you have a slower build-up and the pace is not as fast.'

The intellectual Houllier's post-match press-conferences were keenly anticipated by a jaded media, used to hearing managers run the whole gamut of emotion from 'chuffed' to 'gutted'. Houllier's inaugural briefing was, therefore, something of a letdown. While he may have been struggling to adjust to the frenetic pace of the Premier League, Houllier's summing-up of the match demonstrated that he clearly had no trouble adopting archetypal manager-speak: 'We played well, they played well, we had chances, they had chances, we made mistakes, and so did they, so I think the result was the right one for both teams, even though it wasn't.' Quite.

SEPTEMBER 1998: THE FIRST CRACKS APPEAR

But already the first cracks in the uneasy Houllier–Evans alliance were beginning to appear. Liverpool's unbeaten run was quickly ended by West Ham. Riedle's late consolation at Upton Park could not disguise another flimsy display at the back, with the Reds' central defensive pairing of Staunton and Babb given a torrid afternoon by John Hartson. More pointedly, Houllier and Evans had clashed over how best to utilise Vegard Heggem's talents. Bought primarily as a right-back as the pair's first jointly approved signing, this was the position that Evans felt he should occupy. But while Heggem was clearly adept at getting forward, he already appeared vulnerable as an orthodox defender. Houllier favoured playing him on the right side of midfield with McManaman in a roving 'free' role. The players wondered how two men (particularly two men from as different cultural backgrounds as Houllier and Evans) could be expected to share an identical vision of formation, tactics and team selection. Later Houllier admitted that 'the joint management situation was a problem for the players and the staff. Maybe the players didn't know who was the boss, who they had to refer to.'

Confusion at the training ground translated into uncertainty on the pitch as, in the space of three games in September, Liverpool picked up just one point and that from a fortuitous 3–3 draw against newly promoted Charlton at Anfield. Steve Harkness (roundly abused by the home fans for his indecisive performance), deputising for the injured Paul Ince, was horribly exposed in midfield as the visitors carved out numerous openings. In the space of 90 incident-filled minutes, Charlton reopened all the old wounds that had blighted Liverpool's recent past. The fact that Robbie Fowler scored twice on his comeback from a cruciate knee injury was overshadowed by the visitors' display. The defensive problems that had undermined the fluid attacking play of the past couple of seasons were seemingly no nearer to being solved. Liverpool's solid start to the season had been quickly shattered. Fowler could at least bask in a rousing reception from the home fans. It had not been the same story in the previous season, when the crowd hurled abuse on their favourite son because of his indifferent form and contract demands. The contract issue nevertheless remained unresolved.

Four days after the visit of Charlton, Liverpool lost to arch-rivals Manchester United. McAteer and Bjornebye replaced Staunton and Heggem for the visit to Old Trafford but the defence still looked error-prone. This time the goalkeeper, American Brad Friedel, was the chief culprit. United won 2–0 with plenty to spare, and not for the first time Redknapp and Ince in the centre of midfield were overrun by more mobile and dominant opponents.

If September had been disappointing, things went from bad to worse as autumn wore on. Speculation concerning Steve McManaman's future was continuing to undermine the club. Real Madrid chairman Lorenzo Sanz had publicly confirmed, for the first time, Real's interest in signing McManaman. FIFA regulations would enable Real to sign a pre-contract with McManaman, binding him to the club, six months before the end of his current deal. In other words, McManaman could be formally announced as a Real player as early as January 1999. Liverpool had less than three months to broker a deal, or else face the galling prospect of losing the player they had nurtured from the age of 15, from youth team to England regular, for nothing. Evans said that newspaper reports linking McManaman with Real Madrid had made Liverpool even more determined to keep him. 'We have been in negotiations on a weekly basis trying to sort something out and we are still confident we can do so. We are also talking to Robbie (Fowler). We've got Jamie Redknapp and Michael Owen signed up but it is difficult when you have so many outstanding young players.'

Liverpool could still turn it on when the mood took them, as the 5–1 demolition of Nottingham Forest in torrential rain at Anfield demonstrated. Frustratingly, however, this was an isolated show of strength, owing much to Owen's predatory instincts (he bagged four of the goals, alongside a nonchalantly accepted volley by McManaman, greeted with a shrug almost of indifference by the scorer). Consistency remained as elusive as at any time in the Souness and Evans eras: after the Forest win, Liverpool's title hopes suffered another setback when, with Owen starved of service, they were outplayed by Leicester at Filbert Street, losing 1–0. To add to the Reds' woes, Jason McAteer was sent off shortly before full-time.

The pressure was mounting on Liverpool's dual managers, or more precisely, one half of the duo. In hindsight, Roy Evans must have felt that his position had been considerably weakened when Houllier was brought in as co-manager before the start of the season. It seemed an ill-fated and ill-thought-out appointment from the outset. Had Houllier, fresh from masterminding France's World Cup triumph, simply *replaced* Evans, a line could have been drawn under the *ancien régime*. Evans was the last in a long lineage dating back to Shankly and part of the fabled Boot Room inner sanctum that sought to appoint new managers from within. Perhaps the failure of the Souness era should have led to the Board appointing an 'outsider' before now. As it was, the dual appointment smacked of desperation, fatally compromising the new man's ability to carry out the root and branch revamp of the squad he saw as essential if Liverpool were to move forward. Privately, Houllier realised the relationship was doomed: 'It was difficult for the players in the long run, the players like to be able to refer to one manager. The concept was obviously extremely difficult for them.' The official line from the club was that Evans and Houllier would operate in tandem, and if they encountered problems, they would work them out together. The reality, as everyone saw it, was that any improvement in performance would be viewed as evidence of Houllier's ability, and any worsening of the situation would be an indictment of Evans' work at the club. While there had been no open hostility or disagreement between the two, the consensus had always been that the arrangement would not last and, if results went against them, Houllier would be the one to survive.

NOVEMBER 1998: LIVERPOOL DISINTEGRATE, ROY EVANS RESIGNS

The dénouement was swift in arriving for Evans. On 7 November, unfancied Derby came to Anfield and won 2–1. The following Tuesday, Tottenham – perennial lambs to the slaughter at Anfield – arrived in Merseyside for a League Cup tie sensing the chance of a kill. On a miserable night, in front of a paltry 20,772 spectators, Liverpool played like strangers, passing the ball with trepidation. The players' inaccuracy betrayed lack of confidence rather than technical ineptitude. Before an incredulous home support, Spurs slipped into gear and cruised to a three-goal lead. Three goals! It was unthinkable that Liverpool could surrender so tamely. To add injury to insult, Owen sustained ligament damage as he collided with Spurs' goalkeeper in forcing the ball home for a late consolation goal. As he limped off, an air of despondency descended on Anfield. Inevitably, a chorus of jeers greeted the final whistle.

The day after the humiliating Spurs defeat, reports were circulating suggesting that Houllier could be in sole charge of team affairs before the next game at home to Leeds, with Evans set to be offered another role within the club. Injuries to Owen and McManaman exacerbated the sense of crisis. It was clear from the headlines in the morning's press that the clamour for change was becoming irresistible: 'Evans: the end' and 'Can it get any worse?' declared the red-tops. That evening the *Liverpool Echo* ran the front-page banner headline: 'Evans Set to Quit' and Evans admitted the pressure was getting to him. 'The speculation has been very difficult to live with. I have done this job with honesty and integrity and seeing the club suffer affects me badly.'

Liverpool were now in the bottom half of the Premier League table. Since going top briefly on 9 September after beating Coventry, the Reds had won only once in the Premiership and had also been eliminated from the League Cup. A season that had held so much promise had turned to nought barely three months in. On Thursday, 12 November 1998, lifelong Liverpool supporter Roy Evans bowed to the inevitable and bade farewell to Anfield in a tearful press conference after over 30 years' service as a player, coach and finally manager. Evans left, in chairman David Moores' words, by 'mutual consent' – it is not Liverpool's way to sack managers. He declined an offer to accept another position within the club, reasoning he didn't want to be 'a ghost on the wall – if we're going to give Gérard and this team a chance, I have to walk away'.

Evans left the team in a state of disarray, but arguably in a stronger position than he had found them when he was brought in to replace Graeme Souness midway through the miserable 1993–94 season with the club £10 million in debt from Souness' disastrous dealings in the transfer market and the team playing football a long way short of the expected standards. Still, despite Evans' best efforts, in the intervening years the side had failed to provide a consistent challenge to Manchester United and Arsenal and were in danger of being left too far behind, both on and off the pitch, to ever bridge the rapidly widening chasm that Alex Ferguson and Arsène Wenger were developing from the rest of the pack.

Such was the scale of the task facing Gérard Houllier as he took over sole responsibility for team affairs. His first move was to bring in fellow Frenchman Patrice Bergues as first-team coach. More surprisingly, Houllier also announced that Evans' assistant, Doug Gilmore, who was leaving the club, was to be replaced by the tough disciplinarian and former Liverpool captain, Phil Thompson, who himself had been sacked as assistant manager by Souness in 1992. 'Le Boss', as he was quickly dubbed by the fans, set out his stall in his first programme notes for the match against Leeds. 'After being appointed team manager, I wanted an assistant who had a Liverpool heart. I am delighted to welcome Phil Thompson back to the club.'

At 2 p.m. on Saturday 14 November 1998, the team coach wheeled out of Annie Road through Shankly Gates to a deafening blast of cheers and shrill cries that would not have been out of place in Merseyside some 35 years earlier. Owen, Fowler and McManaman were the city's new pop idols, the John, Paul and George of modern-day Liverpool. The Houllier regime had started in earnest.

The first half against Leeds failed to live up to the bubbling sense of expectation that came with the realisation that a new era was dawning for the club, but Liverpool began the second period brightly and it was no surprise when Fowler stroked home a penalty to put the Reds one up with 20 minutes to play. O'Leary brought on his young substitute, Alan Smith, for his first taste of Premiership action. Barely two minutes later, the Kop was silenced as Smith calmly side-footed an equaliser from the edge of the penalty area with his first touch of the ball. The crowd became agitated, screaming for a free kick as Berger tumbled outside the Leeds box. The referee waved away the appeals and, with the Liverpool players losing all discipline, the visitors broke to the other end of the field. Within seconds, Leeds had countered and the ball was nestling in James' net. It was a lesson that Houllier was to absorb fully – and return to several times in the future as evidence of how his team had matured by contrast with the follies of '98. Hasselbaink added a third for good measure in front of a disbelieving Kop. Three goals in seven minutes: the Reds were in turmoil, and Houllier's task – if it hadn't looked so beforehand – now appeared Herculean. As the supporters filed out, one disgruntled fan muttered 'fortress Anfield' in derision. The future had never seemed more bleak.

Later that week, things took another turn for the worse. McManaman's adviser admitted Real Madrid had made an inquiry about the midfielder, claiming Real were one of about 14 clubs in the running for the Liverpool star. He also insisted that constant speculation was flattering rather than unsettling for McManaman, who would remain committed to Liverpool 'as long as he remained at Anfield'. The comments were not encouraging. Liverpool's offer of a new contract remained on the table but it was doubtful that McManaman was seriously considering it. Barely a week into his reign Houllier was faced with sorting out a contract wrangle that had dragged on for a year, just as the player was preparing to sit out the next two months with a recurring ankle injury. While McManaman stalled on signing a new deal, Houllier's dilemma was to decide whether the player (valued at no less than £12 million) was worth the £50,000-a-week wages he was thought to be demanding to re-sign with Liverpool, or whether the departure of Evans would provide a convenient reason for McManaman to leave Anfield.

The football returned to centre stage but despite a thrilling 4–2 victory at Villa Park against the league leaders courtesy of a vintage Fowler hat trick, the season continued in chaotic and disorderly fashion. The Villa performance was followed by the latest in a series of poor away displays in Europe. Despite taking the lead through Owen, the Reds surrendered abjectly to a stylish, but hardly heavyweight, Celta Vigo side. This second 3–1 reverse in the space of a fortnight was almost too much for Liverpool's older supporters to bear. Brought up on year after year of unbroken domination in Europe until the Heysel tragedy, Liverpool's recent performances on the continent were a pale shadow of their illustrious predecessors'. The Reds' latest European exit bore all the hallmarks of craven defending and careless ceding of possession that had characterised their 3–0 defeats at Strasbourg and Paris St Germain in the previous two campaigns.

The season moved on, minus Europe and with European qualification for next year looking ever less likely. Trouble was brewing behind the scenes as Houllier took his first tentative steps towards what he knew, but would not publicly acknowledge, was set to be a painful rebuilding process.

The Frenchman's first signing, Jean Michel Ferri, was a curio – an unheralded midfield player, pushing 30, from the Turkish First Division. Ferri was, by all accounts, a defensive midfield player in the Paul Ince mode, albeit of rather more modest ability. Why did Houllier sign him? Ferri scarcely set foot on a football pitch in a Liverpool jersey during his brief tenure at the club. He was sold to Sochaux in the close season after a mere two first-team appearances. The rumours persist to this day: Ferri was not bought by Houllier to play football, but as a trusted fellow countryman to be Houllier's eyes and ears in the Liverpool dressing-room, a spy to report back on team unrest as Houllier gradually introduced the tactics and disciplines on and off the field that would bring the glory days back to the club. Central to Houllier's philosophy was the building of team spirit – without it, you were nothing. It would only take one individual, particularly a commanding figure in the dressing-room, to undermine that team spirit and if Houllier's plans were to have any chance of success, the unruly elements of the squad had to be uprooted. The decline had gone on too long; the malaise at the club, allowed to fester under 'Uncle' Roy's indulgent stewardship, was too deeply rooted for Houllier to delay in acting.

And act Houllier did. First, he identified the players that would form the core of his new team. Carragher and Berger were quickly tied to new deals. The nucleus of a strong side was established: Redknapp, Owen, Berger, Matteo and Carragher. Behind the scenes youngsters David Thompson and Steven Gerrard were coming through. But would Robbie Fowler and Steve McManaman still be around next season to form part of that nucleus? It was an issue that would occupy Houllier for the next few months.

While indolence may have crept in among the superstars of the first-team, the club's youth development policy (under Academy Director Steve Heighway) was still second to none. The startling emergence of Michael Owen was testament to that. Now, Houllier was asked to watch the youth players in training at Liverpool's new state-of-the-art Academy in Kirkby. The club's coaching staff had informed him that a talented youth may be ready to make the step up to training with the seniors: Stephen Wright, a tall 18-year-old central defender. Houllier watched – and was impressed. But another, equally gangly, youth stopped him in his tracks. This boy *was* ready to train with the first-team. His confidence and assurance on the ball were remarkable to behold in one so young. Steven Gerrard was on his way to the first-team headquarters at Melwood.

DECEMBER 1998: THE CHRISTMAS PARTY INCIDENT

Saturday, 5 December 1998 was a significant day in Houllier's reign, although it probably did not seem so to anyone outside the manager's inner sanctum at the time: Steven Gerrard was handed his first-team debut by the Frenchman – at right-back, with instructions to quell the threat of Spurs' in-form winger, David Ginola. Not the easiest of starts, and Gerrard struggled manfully all afternoon to cope with Ginola's mazy runs and sharp movement off the ball. Outclassed for nearly an hour, Liverpool almost snatched a point in a grandstand finish after Patrik Berger's free kick curled into the top corner from 25 yards. Houllier bemoaned his team's inability to start playing until they had fallen behind. 'The game is for 90 minutes. We played for 60. In the 30 minutes in between, we lost the match. I shall be asking the players whether they will be happy with two-thirds of their pay this week.' As it was, this second defeat to the North London outfit in less than a month at least marked the beginning of a young man's career that was to have a considerable impact on the upturn in Liverpool's fortunes in the coming seasons.

Liverpool's other teenage wunderkind, Michael Owen, rounded off a 1998 to remember by being crowned BBC's Sports Personality of the Year. The same day he missed a penalty as Liverpool went down to a depressing 1–0 defeat at Wimbledon (their seventh loss in just seventeen Premier League matches). The Christmas period, however, brought much-needed cheer to the squad, with back-to-back victories over Middlesbrough and Newcastle (the latter ending 4–2 after the Reds had gone in at half-time trailing 2–0). But even then, the excitement of the Newcastle comeback was tarnished by unsavoury tabloid revelations of off-field misdemeanours. This time the unlikely figure at the centre of the attention was Jamie Carragher.

The team's Christmas fancy-dress party, held in the basement of a Liverpool bar, had quickly descended into a Dionysian orgy. The *News of the World* newspaper reported that Carragher, dressed as the hunchback of Notre Dame, discarded his hump and clothes and was sprayed with whipped cream by a stripper. Paul Ince, watching with increasing concern, at one stage had to order the drunken Carragher to put down a stripper he had hoisted over his shoulder. As things got out of hand, two other strippers performed lewd acts on Carragher and a friend. A video camera was smashed by security in the ensuing rumpus; a second escaped undetected. At this point, to paraphrase the immortal words of Sid Waddell, things couldn't have got any more exciting had Elvis Presley walked into the bar and ordered a plate of chips. One of the girls spoke about her role in the orgy the following day: 'They were animals. It was like a monkeys' tea party.'

Simian escapades aside, Carragher was quickly forgiven by Houllier after a stern talking-to. In fact, Houllier thought a lot of Jamie Carragher. He admired his passion, his determination to devote his all to the Liverpool cause and the raw talent that had smoothed his path to first-team regular at 21. The Christmas party was an embarrassment to the club, but would be quickly forgotten, and Carragher, a local lad much liked by the staff and squad, could be allowed one youthful indiscretion. Moreover, the party hadn't affected Liverpool's form on the pitch, as the Middlesbrough and Newcastle results demonstrated.

For Gérard Houllier, already plotting the biggest squad overhaul in Anfield history, Christmas was an ideal opportunity for some forward planning. At a late-night Christmas Eve meeting with David Moores, Peter Robinson and other key individuals in the club's hierarchy Houllier drew up his list of transfer targets for the next season – and many startled club officials were surprised to have their Christmas celebrations interrupted by inquiries from Liverpool about players.

JANUARY 1999: McMANAMAN AND THE FA CUP: DOUBLE DISAPPOINTMENT

As the season moved into its second half, Houllier continued to assess the extent of the decline on the playing field. The remainder of the 1998–99 term was a write-off, with Liverpool heading for mid-table mediocrity. Houllier would probably have been content to let the season drift quietly out before wielding the axe on those members of the squad he did not consider to be part of his vision for the future. Liverpool being Liverpool, things were never going to be that straightforward. The two men at the centre of the Reds' best football under Evans, Fowler and McManaman, ensured that Houllier's first term in sole charge did not pass uneventfully.

The new year brought two new blows to Houllier's nascent reign. The first was not a surprise. On 12 January, the inevitable announcement that fans had feared for some time duly arrived. Steve McManaman was to join European Cup holders Real Madrid on a lucrative five-year deal with effect from 1 July, the day after his agreement with Liverpool expired. As McManaman would be a free agent on the expiry of his contract, under the Bosman ruling Liverpool would receive no transfer fee or compensation.

Disappointing though the news was, it was also a relief for Houllier to have the matter resolved once and for all. McManaman was a key player, but also something of a loose cannon in a footballing sense, his meandering dribbles often petering out with scuffed shots or misplaced crosses. The team were also over-reliant on him and frequently ran out of ideas if McManaman was tightly shackled or off his game. Sheffield Wednesday had employed their captain, Peter Atherton, in the previous season as a man marker with instructions to follow the roving McManaman all over the pitch. Their creativity stifled, Liverpool lost 1–0 at Anfield. Other Premiership sides took note and it became the norm for the Reds' playmaker to find himself the main focus of attention for opposing defences.

After the Madrid deal was announced, McManaman came in for some fierce criticism in the media and from sections of Liverpool's supporters. Because Real were getting their man without having to shell out the £12 million rivals Barcelona had been reportedly ready to pay a year previously, they were able to offer McManaman a fantastic financial package. His salary was widely stated to be in the region of £60,000 a week, making him by some distance the highest-paid Englishman in world football and instantly catapulting him into major league status on a par with Europe's other top earners (Del Piero, Ronaldo, Zidane et al). Yet McManaman had been with Liverpool for over ten years and, in that time, had given his all for the club, frequently playing out of his skin in a team that shed goals more frequently than David James changed his hair colour. During the dark years of Souness and Evans, he – along with Robbie Fowler – was Liverpool's shining light. It was McManaman's misfortune to ply his trade in the Premiership at a time when the Mersey giants were living off past glories. The only trophy won by Liverpool during Evans' reign was the low-prestige League Cup in 1995, courtesy of a virtuoso performance, and two goals, by McManaman (a display of wing wizardry no less a figure than Tom Finney likened to Stanley Matthews at his best). Football supporters can be fickle, but generally Liverpool's fans are among the most knowledgeable and appreciative in the country. The majority felt, rightly, that McManaman, just turned 27, had earned the opportunity to test himself among Europe's finest while still at the peak of his career. In truth, there was no immediate prospect of McManaman playing Champions League football in the red shirt of his hometown club. That he was the undoubted beneficiary of the much-maligned Bosman ruling was equally true but to criticise him for holding out for his market-worth was wide of the mark.

The second blow to Houllier came with a heartbreaking defeat to their nemesis Manchester United in the fourth round of the FA Cup and with it, Liverpool's last chance of rescuing their season. Liverpool had a dream start when, with just three minutes played, Michael Owen headed home Heggem's right-wing cross. From then on United piled on the pressure but Liverpool held firm. Then, with barely a minute left and a famous victory beckoning, Liverpool finally cracked. Beckham took a free kick, Cole headed down and Yorke equalised. Seconds later, as the clock moved into stoppage time, the ball fell invitingly to Solskjaer six yards out. He drove past James to seal victory. Houllier was despondent, but vowed revenge: 'I feel disappointed for our players and fans. We haven't beaten United in the Cup for over 70 years, but I assure people that we will beat them at some stage.'

FEBRUARY 1999: THE TAUNTING OF LE SAUX

Victory over one of the Premiership elite still looked a long way off. At Chelsea, Liverpool were sliding to a traditional defeat in an otherwise unremarkable game when Robbie Fowler, who had been involved in a running feud with the Chelsea full-back, Graeme Le Saux, all afternoon (suggesting that Le Saux was indeed 'playing for the other side') took things too far. As Le Saux prepared to take a free kick, Fowler turned his back on him, bent over and gestured provocatively to his rear. The implication was obvious: Le Saux's sexuality was being called into question. Le Saux – long on learning, but short of fuse – responded with an off-the-ball elbow in Fowler's face, unseen by the referee but picked up by the television cameras. The Football Association cited both players for misconduct, Le Saux claiming in his defence that he was reacting to Fowler's taunts and gestures suggesting he was homosexual. Le Saux's off-field image (*Guardian* reader, educated, well spoken) was gleefully contrasted in the press with the working-class, Toxteth upbringing of a man who had once memorably declined an offer to join Le Saux and others on a sight-seeing tour of the Great Wall of China, while on a trip with England, on the grounds that 'once you've seen one wall, you've seen them all'. Once again, Liverpool were being asked to explain the actions of their errant star as the media made capital of the apparent decline in discipline at a once great club. Fowler appeared out of his depth in attempting to explain his actions. Houllier was privately furious, and his temper was not improved by a second controversial episode in quick succession involving his wayward striker.

APRIL 1999: THE COCAINE CELEBRATION

Liverpool's first match at Anfield since the Le Saux incident was the 160th Merseyside derby. There is in the lingua franca of the terraces, 'history' between Fowler and the Everton supporters. Over the past few seasons, Fowler had been ruthlessly baited over unsubstantiated accusations that he had a fondness for taking drugs. His every appearance in Merseyside derbies was the cue for the chanting of 'Smackhead'. In an already highly charged atmosphere Liverpool fell behind barely 30 seconds into the game. Their pride stung, the Reds swarmed forward. Within minutes they had been awarded a penalty at the Anfield Road end in front of the visiting fans. Fowler stepped up to equalise and then, moving before his detractors, celebrated by crawling on all fours along the white line of the six-yard box, pretending to sniff the line as if it were cocaine or heroin. With a ban for the Le Saux incident still hanging over him, a charge of crowd incitement could now be added to Fowler's burgeoning misconduct file. It wasn't long before Fowler was celebrating again, in a more customary fashion, his 100th Anfield goal as he converted from McManaman's flick-on. After Berger had volleyed Liverpool into a 3–1 lead, Everton pulled a goal back and a dramatic match ended with the Reds holding on for victory, Steven Gerrard twice making desperate goalline clearances in the final minutes.

After the match, Houllier invited ridicule by choosing to defend Fowler, claiming he often pretended to sniff the grass in training when practising his goal celebrations: 'He was pretending to graze like a sheep – it's a goal celebration he picked up from Rigobert Song.' In the face of stinging media criticism, Houllier wisely backtracked: 'On Saturday I did not have the benefit of television pictures but, after seeing the video recording of the incident, I realised I was mistaken.' Fowler was forced to issue a public apology and await his fate at an FA disciplinary committee meeting scheduled for 9 April.

The taunting of Le Saux, irritating though the Chelsea player can frequently be on a football pitch, was inexcusable but displayed no more than ignorance, as opposed to maliciousness, on Fowler's part. The Everton penalty celebration, on the other hand, was a frankly witty response to the mindless and cruel chanting of an idiot minority which was a constant slur on Fowler's reputation. Nonetheless, Fowler was predictably castigated for both incidents and Liverpool's season went into a tailspin. Fowler dropped plans to appeal against the six-match ban imposed on him by the FA (two matches for the Le Saux gesture; a somewhat arbitrary four for the cocaine-snorting goal celebration), persuaded to do so by the FA's willingness to let him serve the ban early so that he would not miss any matches at the start of the 1999–2000 campaign. It was a compromise that Liverpool had wanted, but Fowler's riposte, issued through his legal adviser, underlined his disillusionment at his treatment by the FA: 'The penalties were unjustified and harsh. For some time he has been subjected to the vile taunts that he takes drugs. The disciplinary committee appears to have ignored this provocation in imposing a four-match ban and the largest fine ever handed to a player.' (Fowler received a record £34,000 penalty.)

With Fowler missing for the final six games of the season, Liverpool now predictably lost his strike partner, Michael Owen, to a serious hamstring injury sustained in a goalless draw at Elland Road. The team soldiered on, threadbare in attack, wearied by the continual on- and off-field controversies that marred Houllier's first year at the helm. With nothing left but pride to play for, Liverpool took on Manchester United at Anfield and – gaining a small measure of revenge for January's painful FA Cup exit – held the champions elect to a 2–2 draw, after trailing 2–0 with an hour gone. Houllier described it as 'a bloody good result for our supporters. It proves the players have not only the talent and heart, but the passion and commitment.' Still, Paul Ince's leap into an ecstatic Kop to celebrate the equaliser as if it were the winning goal in a Cup final was a sad indictment of Liverpool's underachieving season.

The season closed with Steve McManaman playing his final game in a red shirt at Anfield and sadly, his last before his mother died after a long struggle against cancer. McManaman was substituted before the final whistle to a standing ovation and Liverpool concluded with a 3–0 win and a mid-table finish.

Now, for Houllier, the real work of rebuilding the side could finally begin.

THE CLOSE SEASON: REVOLUTION!

A summer free of international tournaments was the perfect opportunity for Gérard Houllier to build his own team. The priority, clearly, was strengthening a defence that had consistently leaked goals in recent campaigns and was notoriously suspect in the air and on set pieces. Wasting no time, his first key signing of the new era was giant 6ft 4in. Finnish defender Sami Hyypiä from Dutch first division club Willem II in the first week of the summer break. Houllier had been tracking Hyypiä (a virtual unknown outside of Holland) for some time and had heard consistently excellent reports from his scouts. On checking him in person, he and assistant Phil Thompson were both immediately impressed not so much with Hyypiä's imposing defensive abilities (which they had expected) but with his assurance on, and use of, the ball. They had found their man.

The arrival of the impressively built Finn at Anfield brought back memories of Shankly's unveiling of his new centre-half, the 'Red Colossus', Ron Yeats, in 1961. Shankly famously invited reporters to 'take a walk round' the rock upon which he would build his defence. Hyypiä seemed to inspire the calm and sense of dominance that had been missing at Liverpool since the halcyon days of Hansen and Lawrenson. Better still, he could bring the ball out of defence with something approaching the same élan.

Liverpool next agreed a fee of £3.75 million with French side RC Lens for their Czech midfielder Vladimir Smicer, a close friend of compatriot

Patrik Berger. Houllier had been trying to sign Smicer for the previous two months but refused to meet his former club's £10 million valuation of the player. Smicer rejected a move to Paris St Germain to enable Liverpool to continue their pursuit and finally, soon after celebrating his 26th birthday, Vladi was on his way to Merseyside to tie up a deal that would see him become the proud owner of the number seven shirt recently vacated by Steve McManaman. Although not a direct replacement for McManaman, Smicer's brief was to provide the team with a creative hub, linking the more deep-lying midfielders with the attack. He was agile, skilful and two-footed, capable of operating on either flank, or off the strikers in a 4-3-1-2 formation. Despite his undoubted class and versatility, his signing was greeted in the media with some scepticism, the consensus being that Smicer was not the 'name' signing required to fill the void left by McManaman's departure. This was a short-sighted view: Smicer starred for the Czech Republic during their surprise run to the final of Euro '96 and was instrumental in inspiring RC Lens to their first-ever title. Not only was he an accomplished international but, of equal importance to Houllier, he was very much a team player, not something that could always be said of McManaman. In short, he fitted perfectly into Houllier's vision for the new Liverpool.

It was not immediately clear how the next foreign import unveiled to a dubious Merseyside public would fit into this vision. Aboudacar 'Titi' Camara was a burly, Guinean striker plying his trade at another French First Division side, Olympic Marseilles. The Liverpool fans' first glimpse of Camara was not an auspicious one. His cumbersome performance coming on as a substitute in Marseilles' UEFA Cup final defeat to Parma was the cue for widespread groaning and head-shaking at television sets across Liverpool. Nor was their mood lightened by the media's mirthful response to Houllier's peculiar description of Camara as the 'African Overmars'. No matter, the revolution went on apace as Houllier continued to scour the continent for the right players. Houllier's transfer policy was deliberately aimed at developing a team that would grow together in the next five years – the amount of time Houllier felt was needed to turn the club into title winners and a force in Europe again. This was no quick fix; no importing of superannuated stars on inflated salaries looking to see out their days in the rich playground of the Premiership. The players Houllier signed had to be young (26 or under), talented and hungry to play for Liverpool. In an era of corporate footballers, these players had to be prepared to make an emotional investment in the club.

To make way for his new recruits, Houllier needed to clear out the debris of the Roy Evans era. Evans had somehow managed to pick up a ragbag assortment of Scandinavians, journeymen and former Wimbledon players (in the case of Leonhardsen, a combination of all three). Having already sold two players who had never really been up to the required standard, Steve Harkness and Jason McAteer, the latter to Blackburn Rovers for a staggering £4 million, the next two players to depart Anfield would do so making a bigger splash: England internationals David James and Paul Ince. Houllier had been keen to resolve the goalkeeping position for some time. He did not rate either of the men he inherited from Evans – James and Brad Friedel. James had earned himself the epithet 'Calamity' after a series of high-profile blunders, although it was the general air of unease he inspired in his defence, rather than the too-frequent individual errors, that worried Houllier more. James was a gifted keeper who, along with the team generally, had never really fulfilled his potential in recent seasons. So James moved on to pastures new at Villa Park, relishing the chance to relaunch his career.

For Paul Ince, on the wrong side of 30, the situation was rather different. Ince's days at Anfield had looked numbered since Houllier assumed sole control of team affairs in November. Bought from Inter Milan in the summer of 1997, it was widely believed at the time that Ince's arrival at the club would be the trigger for Liverpool to go on and win the Premier League. Ince was supposed to be the final piece in Evans' jigsaw, replacing the ageing John Barnes in central midfield as the defensive anchor and partner for Redknapp. However, Ince's influence had been more keenly felt in the Liverpool dressing-room than on the pitch. He was the central figure in a cabal of established stars who were none too impressed by the new disciplinary code and training regime brought into the club by Houllier and Thompson. Houllier, for his part, viewed Ince as a disruptive influence on team spirit and as having a potentially destabilising effect on the new order he was instigating at Anfield. If Ince had been delivering the goods on the pitch, he may have been able to convince Houllier of his worth, but it is unlikely. As it was, Houllier saw Ince's position as midfield anchor as particularly critical, and one for which he was prepared to spend, if necessary, the majority of the £20 million war chest earmarked for the summer's rebuilding programme. Ince became increasingly marginalised at Anfield after the players reported back for pre-season training at the beginning of July. After several stories had circulated in the media about his availability, he sought clear-the-air talks with Houllier and was told, in no uncertain terms, that his future lay away from Anfield. Ince was not involved in Liverpool's Swiss training camp and stayed behind to arrange his £1 million move to Middlesbrough.

The departure of Ince was a pivotal moment for Houllier. He had taken on the biggest figure in the dressing-room and shown him the door and, in the process, earned the respect of supporters who realised Houllier was at Liverpool for the long haul. On his departure, Ince, his ego bruised, launched a savage attack on Houllier, helpfully clarifying his place of birth in the process: 'I want Houllier to get the sack and take Thompson down with him. He comes from France (!) and I can't even believe he's managed a team before because he certainly doesn't seem to know how to.' Ince also claimed he would drag the club down (a little over two years later Houllier, clearly still irked by Ince's remarks, noted acidly that he had indeed dragged Liverpool down – to three Cup finals in the space of nine months in Cardiff!).

Houllier, professorial of image, with the air of a kindly uncle, possessed an iron fist (if need be) inside the velvet gloves that were steering Liverpool into calmer waters. 'I did what I had to do. I felt some things had to change. I would still do that if I thought it was needed. To me the worst is when a player is a cheat. When he says, "I give my all for the fans" and I know that behind the scenes, he's doing everything wrong. To me that's a betrayal to the fans, the club, his team mates. That's my main target. To get rid of him. I hate players who say the right things in the press and then do the wrong things. When I am aware of that, he's in danger. He's in great danger.' Liverpool had found their toughest manager since Shankly. He was rapidly on the way to becoming their most respected too.

With Ince gone, Houllier moved to fill the holding-midfielder vacancy.

With the new season barely a fortnight away, he concluded his all-foreign summer spending spree with the purchase of Newcastle United's German international Dietmar Hamann for a club record transfer fee of £8 million. Hamann, a former Bayern Munich player, was of proven class and, like all Houllier's signings, at 26 young enough to play a major role in Houllier's five-year plan for the club.

With the dependable Swiss centre-half, Stéphane Henchoz, brought in from Blackburn to partner Sami Hyypiä and Sander Westerveld, the Dutch number two goalkeeper to Edwin Van Der Sar, arriving from Vitesse Arnhem for a British transfer record for a goalkeeper (£3.6 million), Houllier was able to unveil a full complement of six new signings – all of them foreign – before the season's curtain raiser: a friendly tournament in Ireland. Houllier was roundly criticised in the media for failing to buy British in his revamp of the team. The criticism missed the mark on two counts: not only were high-quality British players so scarce as to be priced out of the domestic market, but Houllier's signings were brought in to complement a strong, young English (mainly Liverpudlian) core. 'I see no problem with a foreign player in this country,' retorted Houllier, 'as long as he brings more quality to the team he is in. I think a lot of English players could say they have benefited from performing alongside top international players. Take David Beckham and Eric Cantona. I am happy to buy English players but managers often ask crazy prices for them. This is usually why a manager looks to the continent to strengthen his squad.'

Throughout his ongoing metamorphosis of the club, Houllier always stressed the importance of maintaining a 'Liverpool Heart' to his team and, good as his word, announced that Liverpool's new club captain, taking over from Paul Ince for the 1999–2000 season, would be the long-serving Jamie Redknapp. Robbie Fowler, surprisingly, was named as the new vice-captain, with Houllier hoping that the added responsibility incumbent in the role would help his tearaway striker stay on the straight and narrow.

The first phase of Houllier's rebuilding was complete: the backbone of the side had undergone major surgery. From the goalkeeper through the two centre-backs to the defensive shield in front of them, he had used his expert knowledge of European football to forge what he hoped would be the basis for a settled defensive diamond of strength and cohesion. At last, Liverpool would be able to compete with a spine of iron running through the core of the team in the manner of Houllier's model French national side. Liverpool fans, although apprehensive about how the new signings would gel, could hardly wait for the new season to begin.

3

You'll Never Walk Alone (1999–2000 Season)

Although it was ultimately to end in disappointment, when Liverpool, having seemingly hoisted themselves into the Champions League, disintegrated as triumph beckoned, failing to win – even to score – in their last five games, 1999–2000 was the season the Reds, their pride restored by Gérard Houllier, signalled their re-emergence as a significant force in English football. Gone were the off-field misdemeanours that had characterised the previous year (perhaps partly helped by Robbie Fowler's sidelining with injury for the majority of the campaign). Gone, too, was the comic-book defending for which Liverpool had become renowned in the '90s, as Gérard Houllier won plenty of admirers – if no trophies – in his first full season in sole charge.

Initially, the portents were not good. Three games into the season and Gérard Houllier's best-laid plans had come unstuck. Record signing Dietmar Hamann limped off 30 minutes into the opening match after sustaining ankle ligament damage, forcing Houllier to pitch the raw Steven Gerrard into the fray in central midfield. Michael Owen was still nursing the hamstring injury he had picked up at Leeds in April. The new signings were, understandably, taking time to find their feet. And Houllier's new-look team had lost two of those opening three fixtures, including, embarrassingly, the first home game of the season to newly promoted Watford. In fact, Liverpool had played like strangers, Houllier claiming afterwards that he 'did not recognise' his team (nor, clearly, did his players, judging from the number of passes to players in Watford shirts). Before the match, the Hornets' manager Graham Taylor had handed Houllier a £50 bottle of Château Lagrange 1988, commemorating a vintage title-winning year for Liverpool. It presumably went uncorked after the game.

Needing a victory to calm the early-season nerves, Liverpool returned to Elland Road – the scene of Owen's injury – amidst talk in the media of impending crisis. Liverpool, under Houllier, seemed to be developing a peculiar affinity with Leeds. Games against the Yorkshire outfit were inextricably linked to key events in Houllier's stewardship as Liverpool manager (his first match in sole charge, the Owen injury, the occasion of his dramatic collapse and dash to hospital) and his team were frequently bracketed with O'Leary's 'babies' as the rising force of English football. On this occasion, the Reds quickly fell a goal behind but held their nerve to produce a coherent display of slick pass-and-move football, eventually running out 2–1 winners, with Titi Camara silencing a few of the doubters with a stunning first-time volley to set them on their way.

The breathing space afforded by the Leeds victory meant Liverpool could approach the potentially awkward encounter with Arsenal in upbeat mood and, buoyed by Robbie Fowler's best performance thus far in Houllier's time at the club, won comfortably. With Steven Gerrard settling in well in midfield, it appeared that Houllier's newly assembled team was starting to take shape.

Unfortunately, before they could build any momentum, Liverpool were rocked back on their heels by successive home defeats to Manchester United and Everton. The United game was ill-tempered throughout (Cole was sent off, Beckham lucky not to be, after stamping on Redknapp) and a personal disaster for Jamie Carragher who succeeded in twice putting the ball into his own net as United sailed into a 3–1 lead. Westerveld, appearing mesmerised by his first experience of the mayhem engendered by a Liverpool–United encounter, stayed firmly rooted to his line as Beckham swung over a series of dangerous crosses in the first-half. Houllier blasted his players at half-time: 'I know what's going wrong. We're fearing the low crosses too much and defending too deep, instead of pushing up and leaving space for the goalkeeper to come out.' Despite a spirited second-half showing, the Reds were left to rue their defensive blunders. 'If you make mistakes against United, you pay cash,' Houllier said afterwards. Presumably, Liverpool had long since negotiated an overdraft facility for that particular account. Back at Melwood, Westerveld was encouraged by the coaching staff to take a more pro-active stance. This he did in the next few matches, coming for crosses and corners with the zeal of a religious convert, although initially he succeeded only in creating panic among his own defenders. He would soon settle down.

The Merseyside derby, like the United game, was a tempestuous affair, Liverpool losing their cool after failing to claw back Everton's early strike. Westerveld and Gerrard were both sent off, the latter for a reckless assault on Kevin Campbell. Michael Owen was fortunate not to join them for launching himself into a dreadful two-footed lunge on David Weir after losing control of the ball. In the aftermath of the defeat, Gérard Houllier moved swiftly to clamp down on the ill-discipline, which, added to Liverpool's lengthening injury list, was threatening to undermine their season before it had got properly underway. He accused his team of 'losing the plot, losing control and losing their cool', explaining to his players that 'you have got to maintain self-control in such situations, you have got to play with your brain'. Houllier took Michael Owen to one side to spell out the need to curb a reckless streak that had brought him a red card at Old Trafford two seasons earlier. 'I've spoken to Michael about what happened,' said Houllier. 'I have to admit I was a bit ashamed after the Everton game because the players took things too far. They were desperate to beat Everton and were getting frustrated with how the game was going. But their passion has to be channelled in the right direction and I have made that clear to them.'

The embattled Houllier, just eight matches into the campaign (four of them lost), was coming under increasing pressure to restore stability and cure the defensive problems that continued to bedevil his team's chances of stringing a consistent run of results together. Houllier, in turn, was agitated by the disruption caused to his plans by the numerous injuries to his squad, particularly his summer signings, that had left him unable to field his first-choice team thus far. Desperate to kick-start Liverpool's season, he was prepared to risk playing the likes of Dietmar Hamann, Vladimir Smicer, Stéphane Henchoz, and even Michael Owen and Robbie Fowler, through their injuries and rehabilitation programmes. 'These players have missed our pre-season,' Houllier said, 'they have missed games and they are unfit.

But if they don't play they will stay unfit. They now have to play. We now must have our best players out there. Some are not up to Premier League fitness, but we will have to push them and play them.'

That Liverpool's stricken stars were being asked to battle through the pain barrier to salvage the club's season was indicative of Houllier's growing, though unfounded, concern that he was not going to be given the time to implement the carefully mapped-out five-year plan he saw as essential to revitalise the team's fortunes. His determination to field his best side at all costs was in marked contrast to the more measured rotational policy he felt able to adopt a little over a year later. But by then, the squad had been bolstered further and Houllier felt he had the depth of talent to rest players or omit them for tactical reasons, without jeopardising his team's chances of success. By then, too, the team's progress had given him the confidence to back his own judgment – in even the most controversial selections.

In the midst of this mini-crisis, fuelled mainly by media overreaction to the early defeats, the Liverpool hierarchy stood firm, Peter Robinson assuring Houllier that he had the board's complete backing. Having invested heavily over the summer in recruiting the players that Gérard felt were right for the club, there was never any question that the manager would receive anything other than the unswerving loyalty of the board. In any event, Robinson, David Moores and fellow key board members such as Rick Parry believed unreservedly in Houllier's vision, echoing the sentiments of France's new coach, Roger Lemerre, who publicly backed his fellow countryman: 'Liverpool's squad needed major surgery. Changes had to be made and Gérard has been decisive in who he has let go and brought in. He is an excellent judge of a player.' A handful of defeats altered nothing, particularly given that injuries to established stars, as well as to several of the new signings, had hampered progress so far. Houllier was realistic, recognising that his much-changed squad needed time to develop, even if his patience was not unlimited: 'I have always said it would take time to get things right. In the end, it may mean that we need other players to get what we want. But at first, any changes to the team will be made from within the squad. If that were not to solve things then changes will come from outside.'

The upsurge in Liverpool's fortunes under Houllier, which was to vindicate the board's support, began in low-key mode with a hard-fought 0–0 draw at Aston Villa. Significantly, the game marked the long-awaited Premiership entrance of Stéphane Henchoz (even though he had not yet fully recovered from a summer hernia operation) as Sami Hyypiä's partner in the centre of defence. For the first time under Houllier, the backbone of his newly fashioned side – Hyypiä, Henchoz and Hamann – had played together, and with an immediate impact, as Liverpool's defence went unbreached despite the team having to play the majority of the match with ten men.

The workmanlike goalless draw at Villa Park was the beginning of a notable improvement in form, as Liverpool embarked on a remarkable sequence of just two defeats in 26 league matches, a run stretching over seven months. Throughout this period, Houllier was able to field a settled defence, pairing Henchoz and Hyypiä in the middle of the back four in virtually every game, with Hamann 'sitting' in Houllier's favoured anchor role just in front of them. Only 16 goals were conceded over the course of those 26 matches, by some distance the best defensive record in the league and eloquent testimony to the quality of Houllier's reshaped defence.

The team's measured, rather than spectacular, progress – more Ingmar Bergman than Ingrid Bergman – was most evident in the newfound discipline displayed in games that previously might have ended in defeats or draws. In recent seasons, Liverpool had often struggled to break down the massed defences of lower or mid-table opposition visiting Anfield, becoming frustrated in the process and frittering away points in consequence as their play became increasingly ragged. Now, in home games against Bradford and Sheffield Wednesday, Liverpool quickly fell behind, but rather than panic, kept their shape, confident that, provided they played their natural game, their superior football would prevail, and, as a result, won both games comfortably. The Sheffield Wednesday match was memorable, too, for the part played in the victory by Liverpool's rising stars, Thompson, Gerrard and Murphy, all of whom scored fine goals. Gerrard's performance in particular was outstanding, as he tackled ferociously and drove the team forward in a manner that belied his tender years. He was more than repaying Houllier's faith in him; a belief that had seen the Liverpool manager jettison the experienced Paul Ince in pre-season and now, in the wake of Jamie Redknapp's latest injury set-back, decline to enter the transfer market in order to buy a big-name replacement.

Liverpool produced another focused and patient performance against Derby to commemorate the first anniversary of Houllier's appointment as sole manager, running out 2–0 winners after the game had appeared destined for a goalless draw. Houllier was delighted by the team's progress: 'A year ago we probably wouldn't have won a game like this one against Derby. Remember how we were against Leeds that day? We were one up, and our defenders were arguing in the box with the referee as Leeds equalised and went on to win the match. We are a different team now.'

The most memorable performances in the Reds' slow, but inexorable, climb up the table were the back-to-back wins over Champions League rivals Leeds United and Arsenal in February, Liverpool's only games in a barren six-week spell, the consequence of being knocked out early from both domestic cup competitions and a rare failure to qualify for Europe. The Leeds game was a thriller, punctuated by three stunning long-range strikes by Reds' players. The pick of the bunch was a rasping 25-yard drive by Patrik Berger, so good that the referee, Mike Reed, decided to join in the celebrations! Berger was in a rich vein of goalscoring form, which was just as well, considering that Liverpool, in the continued absence of Fowler and Owen, were forced to pair youth-team player Jon Newby up front, alongside the prodigiously untalented Erik Meijer (the man who disarmingly said on his eventual transfer: 'It's crazy, really, paying so much money for a footballer of my qualities'). Still, whatever his limitations as a player (and he never managed to score a league goal in his time on Merseyside), Meijer's brief turn in the Anfield spotlight was cherished by Liverpool's fans for his passionate – and obvious – love for the club, and refusal to acknowledge the concept of a 'lost cause'. Many a game's final ten minutes were enlivened by a cameo substitute appearance from Erik Meijer, charging around the pitch like a half-crazed Nordic raider in the middle of a particularly gruesome pillaging expedition. Opposition defenders were suitably unnerved by his presence, but Meijer's unstinting efforts reflected Liverpool's progress under Houllier in the 1999–2000 season. The team played with a tigerish passion not seen from the Reds in years, throwing themselves wholeheartedly into tackles, harrying the opposition all over the pitch, hunting in pairs to dispossess the man with the ball. Their devotion to the cause was total, exemplified by Titi Camara choosing to play for the injury-ravaged Reds, only hours after learning of his father's death. 'You'll Never Walk Alone' had never sounded more apposite.

At Highbury in February, Liverpool needed all these qualities of resilience and team spirit to repel Arsenal after taking an early lead through Camara (created by a sublime Gerrard pass). From then on, the Liverpool defence, marshalled by Hyypiä and Henchoz, held firm. The victory took Liverpool above Arsenal into the giddy heights of third. A coveted Champions League place was now within their grasp.

Three inactive weeks after their visit to Highbury, Liverpool finally emerged from their self-inflicted mid-winter cocoon boasting the services of a new player, prised at great cost from Martin O'Neill's perennial over-achievers, Leicester City. Weighing in at a cool £11 million, Gérard Houllier's first English signing polarised opinion on Merseyside. The 21-year-old Emile Heskey had never been a prolific goalscorer in his time at Filbert Street, but he allied strength and pace to no little skill. Houllier had long been an admirer of his attributes, having first spotted Heskey's potential playing alongside Michael Owen in an England Under-18 international in 1996. 'I didn't know then that one day I would be working for Liverpool, but Emile scored a goal, and I began to follow him. I had Sky at home in France, and Leicester were having some success, so I saw quite a bit of him. Then when I came to Liverpool I mentioned him because I felt we needed some strength and power up front.' In fact, Liverpool had, some months before, agreed a deal that would take Heskey to Anfield for £9 million in the close season. However, with qualification for a lucrative Champions League place depending on the final two months of the season and Owen and Fowler struggling to overcome injuries, Houllier moved to bring the deal forward, knowing that mid-table Leicester, having just won the League Cup, could be persuaded to part with their star striker earlier than agreed. Heskey's premature arrival, however, came at a premium, an additional £2 million, which meant the deal smashed Liverpool's existing transfer record.

Heskey made an immediate impact on his first outing against Sunderland, cutting inside from the right to earn Liverpool a penalty – duly converted by Berger – only three minutes into the match. However, the team were unable to capitalise on their flying start and had to settle for a point from a 1–1 draw. Houllier was quick to pay tribute to his latest signing: 'I was particularly pleased with the way the fans took to Emile immediately. They began singing his nickname, "Bruno", straight away and made him feel very welcome. I felt it was a great debut by Emile and he showed many good attributes. He only trained with the squad for the first time yesterday yet, within a couple of minutes today, he had won a penalty.'

For the visit of Aston Villa three days later, Houllier was able to pair Heskey and Owen together for the first time, the latter making his first start for two months. The combination proved fruitless, as Liverpool were held to a goalless draw, with Owen missing a first-half penalty and Heskey incurring the wrath of Villa manager John Gregory for his apparent inability to stay on his feet: 'He has done it again – he's a cheat. I think he cons referees too many times with the way he hits the deck. He does fall over an awful lot and I think he must have brought his roller-skates with him when he signed from Leicester.' Houllier was not impressed with Gregory's comments, retorting 'his attack was not only unfair but it was unprofessional too. He usually has something to say for himself but I would certainly defend Emile against those sort of accusations.'

Houllier was more concerned that, based on his assessment of the Villa match, his players were going to find it difficult to keep their patience as they entered the final, crucial games of the season. 'Sometimes we are a little bit too hurried in our play and our passes are not measured enough. But I shouldn't be too critical of the team. You have to take into account the age of the side and that some players are just coming back from injury.'

On returning from an appearance as a guest speaker at the Football Expo in Cannes, Houllier was at pains to stress that two of his stars were staying put. In the wake of Heskey's arrival, rumours predictably resurfaced linking Robbie Fowler with a move (to Leeds), and Jamie Redknapp was also reported to be on the verge of leaving Anfield in the near future. 'I need to reassure all the supporters that Robbie and Jamie are not for sale,' Houllier said. 'We are in the process of constructing a squad that can compete with the best and you do not sell your best assets.' A key figure in Liverpool's boardroom *was* leaving, however: Vice-Chairman Peter Robinson announced on Houllier's return from France that he would be retiring from the club on 30 June. Although the move had been widely predicted (drawing to a close a period of transition set in motion two years earlier when Robinson began grooming Rick Parry as his successor), the timing of the departure was still something of a shock. Peter Robinson had been a wonderful servant to Liverpool FC and was held in high regard by not only his colleagues but also the club's supporters. He had, of course, played an instrumental role in bringing Houllier to Liverpool in the summer of 1998. Nonetheless, Robinson's decision to leave at the end of the season did not alter the manager's position at the club. Houllier enjoyed a good relationship with David Moores and Rick Parry, both of whom were supportive of Houllier's plans. Indeed, the board had already earmarked a further £10 million for the ongoing squad rebuilding he had planned for the summer, regardless of whether or not the team succeeded in reserving their seat at the high table of European football – the Champions League.

Ensuring his side qualified for Europe's premier competition was, of course, precisely the reason why Gérard Houllier had asked the board to sanction the purchase of Emile Heskey earlier than planned. But Heskey was by no means the finished article and Houllier realised that the raw edges needed to be smoothed down if he was to get a quick return on his money in the shape of a top-three finish. Heskey's poor goalscoring record, which at Leicester had attracted considerable criticism, remained a heated source of debate among his new club's supporters. It seemed odd that a man with such obvious physical attributes – pace, height, power, possessing of a powerful shot and the ability to surge past defenders at will – should struggle not so much to score goals as to even *look* like scoring goals. Partly through a predilection for drifting into wide positions, Heskey was rarely able to find openings in matches, while in contrast the ball appeared positively attracted to Fowler once he entered the penalty area, like iron filings to a magnet. Gérard Houllier, although excited by Heskey's potential, was aware of the need to develop his game and improve his goalscoring ratio, assuring the supporters that he would transform Heskey into the complete striker: 'I want Emile to score more goals and it is an area I intend working on with him,' he said. 'We don't have time to concentrate on it at the moment, but I know how we will go about it. Robbie Fowler has had to work on his build-up play, and that was done in training as well as by talking to the player. We will work like that with Emile. First, he has to bed in with the rest of the team and get used to our style of play. I will make sure that he develops into more of a penalty-box player. He has already demonstrated that he can lay on chances for others. By the time we have finished working with him, he will be getting on the end of plenty.'

For a while, things progressed smoothly. Following the Villa draw, Liverpool won five matches in a row, the goals being shared around by Owen, Camara and Heskey. The team were now poised to claim the last remaining Champions League place. For Houllier, determined to bring those famous European nights back to Anfield, such as he had witnessed in the '70s and '80s, qualification was imperative: 'If we are to achieve something this season, then we have to get into the European places. We have come a long way now. Mentally and physically we are stronger but it will mean nothing if we finish out of the European spots. Our squad is stronger than last year which proves there is a general progression. But that's not enough. I think we can do a lot better. This is not some kind of unrealistic demand.'

Heskey's early arrival was supposed to be the insurance that Liverpool needed in the event that injury continued to deprive them of Owen and Fowler. As it transpired, Owen played intermittently while Fowler, patently some way short of match fitness, was only thrown into the fray at the season's climax. The onus for scoring the goals that would take the club into the Champions League was therefore thrust, in the main, on Heskey's broad shoulders. Alas, Liverpool's record signing failed to deliver the cutting edge Houllier had been banking on, as Liverpool's form fell away alarmingly. Needing only five points from their remaining five fixtures, the possibility of failing to qualify appeared as remote as a member of REM being arrested for air rage. But the Reds mustered just two points, failing to score even a solitary goal in the process. In consequence, Liverpool narrowly missed out on a Champions League place, having to settle for fourth in the table and the less alluring trappings of the UEFA Cup.

For Houllier, the collapse had an unfortunate precedent. In 1993, Houllier's French team had needed just one point from two home games to qualify for the World Cup but notoriously contrived to lose both. This latest set-back hurt Houllier as much as, if not more than, his failure with the national side. After putting together such an impressive sequence of results, the inability to beat Southampton, Bradford and Leicester in a very manageable-looking run-in was as baffling as it was dispiriting. The team had run out of steam when it mattered most, struggling to create clear goalscoring opportunities and rarely looking like scoring in those final five matches. Still, once the dust had settled, Houllier and his players had plenty to be proud of. Several areas of improvement from the previous year could be clearly traced: Liverpool's defence had been transformed, as Houllier had promised it would, into one of the toughest and most efficiently organised in the league; standards in discipline off the field had risen sharply; and several of the younger players – Murphy, Carragher, Thompson and, above all, Gerrard – had made great strides under Houllier's watchful eye. These developments augured well for the future, and even if the side had not quite achieved the promised land of a Champions League berth, it was perhaps a blessing in disguise, given that the Houllier revolution was still some way short of developing a team able to tackle the demands of a tough Champions League programme. The UEFA Cup would serve as an ideal stepping stone, providing an evolving team with some much-needed European experience while allowing Houllier to focus on improving domestic league form.

The board were certainly impressed by the progress made during the first chapter of Gérard Houllier's reign and, mindful of their man's rising profile, in June Houllier was offered, and signed, a new, improved contract that made him the best-paid manager in England and tied him to the club for the next five years. The season was not yet over for Gérard – he was now off to Euro 2000 to take up his post on UEFA's technical committee, monitoring the performances of Europe's best players in Holland and Belgium. Liverpool, too, were well represented at the tournament: Owen, Heskey, Fowler and Gerrard were all with Kevin Keegan's England squad (Gerrard having broken into the national side in his first full season at Anfield); Smicer and Berger were present with the Czech Republic; Hamann and Markus Babbel, who had already agreed to join Houllier's revolution for the start of next season on a free transfer from Bayern Munich, were with Germany, and Westerveld was with co-host Holland. By the time summer had drawn to a close, Liverpool could boast of two new recruits with Euro 2000 experience behind them: Christian Ziege and Nick Barmby, although neither transfer was to prove straightforward. Gérard Houllier was about to learn that you cannot expect anything less if you ask a player to 'change religion' on Merseyside or to activate a get-out clause in a Middlesbrough player's contract.

4

Liverpool's Tactics Under Houllier

'Counter-attacking is to Liverpool, what Catholicism is to the Pope or communism to the North Korean leader Kim Jong II.' The Spanish newspaper *El Pais*, previewing Barcelona vs. Liverpool in the Champions League.

France under Aimé Jacquet, with Gérard Houllier as technical director, won the World Cup playing with modern football's variation on the classic 4-4-2 theme. The side was built around two defensive central midfielders, Petit and Deschamps, with the attributes necessary to power the engine-room of the team: physical, aggressive and dynamic, but with the skill on the ball to start attacks in the same instant that they broke up those of their opponents. Didier Deschamps, famously derided by Eric Cantona as a 'water carrier', was the man charged with breaking up the flow of the opposition attacks and protecting his back four. Alongside him, the more mobile Emmanuel Petit combined the role of defensive shield with a licence to drive forward into the opposition half. The other, more celebrated, members of France's high-quality midfield quartet, Zinedine Zidane and Youri Djorkaeff, provided the creative impetus. Although a variety of wide players were tried during the tournament (Diomede, Boghossian and Henry), none were particularly successful and ultimately the French success in winning the World Cup was primarily due to the central strength of the midfield and centre backs, with the full backs mainly responsible for providing the team's width. Indeed, one of Jacquet's major selection dilemmas during the tournament was whether to play two or three defensive midfielders (usually Christian Karembeu ahead of winger Thierry Henry).

Playing a 'narrow' midfield requires full-backs who are effectively able to operate as wing backs, albeit as part of a back four. Unsurprisingly, few full-backs in world football have the attacking and defensive qualities to fulfil both roles to a high standard. The 1998 World Cup final was contested between two sides whose full-backs could do just that: France had Thuram and Lizarazu; Brazil boasted Cafu and the turbo-charged Roberto Carlos. The French full-backs, however, were better defensively than their South American counterparts.

So strong was the spine of the French side (Blanc and Desailly in central defence, Petit and Deschamps as their 'protectors') and so excellent the attacking support provided by Lizarazu and Thuram that, once the world's best player was added to the mix (Zidane), it became possible for the team to win the World Cup without fielding a striker of international quality. Remarkably, Newcastle's fans were bemoaning the signing of French forward Stéphane Guivarc'h before his arrival on Tyneside as a World Cup winner. His abject performance at the Stade de France showpiece confirmed that their pessimism was not misplaced. France won the final courtesy of two set-piece goals from Zidane and a last-minute breakaway from Petit. Goals were harder to come by during the knock-out stages of the competition. France failed to score against Italy in the quarter-final but won on penalties. In the second round it was defender Laurent Blanc who scored the 'golden goal' in the 1–0 extra-time victory against Paraguay while full-back Thuram was responsible for both strikes in the 2–1 win over Croatia in the semi-final.

If defence was the basis upon which France's World Cup success was built then, by comparison, Liverpool's defenders appeared in 1998 to be permanently auditioning for the lead role in *The Comedy of Errors*. By then, of course, the tactical mastermind of that French triumph had already been approached by David Moores and Peter Robinson to move in to English club football management as co-manager with Roy Evans for the start of the 1998–99 season. Gérard Houllier brought with him a new tactical approach and a resolve to rebuild Liverpool's crumbling fortress from the very foundations upwards. Houllier's signature signings – Hyypiä and

Henchoz – redefined defending at a club where it appeared to have become a lost art. The revolution at Anfield was not simply about strengthening the defence, however: Houllier felt that Liverpool needed to learn a whole new style of play if they were to achieve consistent success in the future.

Central to Houllier's football philosophy was the concept of 'possession with progression'. Houllier stressed to his players that while possession in and of itself was important, the team must be able at some point to move forward and develop scoring chances from that possession. Houllier's training sessions at Melwood focused on the importance of combination play (one-twos; three-man 'triangle' combinations), cut-backs when crossing the ball on goal and shooting. Liverpool under Evans were famed for their passing game, building up slowly from the back with the centre-halves happy to move the ball sideways until space opened up. The team nearly always eschewed the long ball or direct approach. On a good day Liverpool were the most entertaining side in the Premiership, although their approach play could be painstaking at times and they frequently appeared to be engaged in world-record attempts for the most number of passes played without achieving a shot on goal. Chief culprits John Barnes and Steve McManaman were, of course, by Houllier's first full season in charge, no longer at Anfield.

In marked contrast to the free-flowing, intricate passing of the Roy Evans era, Houllier's Liverpool were a side built more on steel than silk, with an emphasis on moving the ball forward quicker and with greater purpose. The signing of Emile Heskey gave Liverpool an old-fashioned target man to aim long balls at as a variation on the shorter passing game, as well as plenty of pace to aid the quick counter-attacking tactics favoured by Houllier in away matches and, even at times, at Anfield. It was the arrival of Dietmar Hamann, however, which was probably the pivotal signing of the Houllier era. Hamann was drafted in to play in the key midfield anchor role, shielding the defence and breaking up attacks in the manner of Deschamps for France. Alongside him, Steven Gerrard's emergence, in the absence of the injury-prone Redknapp, as a vibrant, driving central midfielder meant that Houllier had the solid foundation upon which to build his new-look team. Not that Liverpool's new style was always easy on the eye, particularly when the Reds were in the process of grinding out 0–0 draws in Europe en route to winning the 2001 UEFA Cup. (The BBC were not best pleased. Having lost out on screening the Champions League, they invested heavily in following Liverpool's travails in Europe only to find viewers switching off faster than horrified ITV executives watching Andy Townsend's laboured efforts at analysis in *The Premiership*'s short-lived *Tactics Truck*.)

The most famous, or rather infamous, of these displays took place at the Nou Camp in the UEFA Cup semi-final against Barcelona. Gérard Houllier, revealing either a neat line in pre-match psychology or particularly black humour, predicted the match would 'be like a table tennis game. Barça like to attack and so do we. I'd be surprised if it ended 0–0.' Cue 90 minutes of almost unrelieved tedium, in which a Barça side boasting the attacking talents of Luis Enrique, Overmars, Kluivert and Rivaldo were restricted to barely a shot at goal worthy of the name. Anyone who witnessed Liverpool's impression of human sandbags at the Nou Camp would have great difficulty in appreciating the table tennis analogy, still less Houllier's claim that his side liked to attack. For Liverpool's fans, compared to the Reds' forays into Europe under Evans, it was a joy to behold. Not so the media. After the match, Spanish and even English journalists were critical of Houllier's tactics. Johann Cruyff accused Liverpool of playing 'anti-football'; Houllier simply told the assembled press corps his objective had been achieved and Barcelona could make their own arrangements. A fortnight later, the scars had still not healed as Barça arrived on Merseyside for the return leg. Philip Cocu claimed 'of the English teams, we would have liked to have played Manchester United or Arsenal. I don't know a lot of teams that play like Liverpool do – with two faces.' Such criticism was music to Houllier's ears.

By the 2001–02 season, Gérard Houllier's Liverpool had refined their tactical approach to almost automative efficiency and Houllier would have to get used to dealing with condemnation of his tactics and his team's counter-attacking style, some of it merited, some betraying a deep misunderstanding of what he was trying to achieve at Anfield. A three-week period in the autumn of 2001 provided examples of both. In Liverpool's inaugural Champions League campaign, the Reds were again drawn with Barcelona. In the first-group match at Anfield, the Catalonians staged a master-class of pass and move football that, at times, left Liverpool chasing shadows. Media criticism of the Reds after such an exhibition by Rivaldo and co was churlish in the extreme. In fact, Barça's second-half display was a perfect model for what Houllier was trying to achieve with his young and talented side – defending, soaking up pressure, keeping and passing the ball with precision, launching blistering counter-attacks at pace and carving open the opposition defence with intricate combination play. Marc Overmars' concluding goal (in Barça's 3–1 win) came at the end of an uninterrupted 24-pass sequence which was warmly applauded by an appreciative Kop.

What frustrated Liverpool's fans more was the team's apparent reluctance to press forward against patently inferior opponents. Either side of Barcelona's visit to Anfield, Liverpool visited mid-table Premiership sides Blackburn and Derby, and on both occasions failed to turn manifest superiority and early one-goal leads into anything resembling a coherent attacking performance. In both games, an overly cautious approach, sitting back and defending deep with an over-reliance on hopeful long balls aimed at Heskey to relieve the pressure, invited disaster. Against Blackburn, two points were dropped, against Derby only Jerzy Dudek's last-minute penalty save preserved Liverpool's fortuitous 1–0 lead. After the Ewood Park clash, former Liverpool manager Graeme Souness, now in charge at Blackburn, could not hide his displeasure at Liverpool's tactics: 'There's no comparison between the teams I played in and the Liverpool teams of today. I don't really want to expand on that other than to say we kept possession and they kept possession. The difference was that we kept the ball a lot higher up the pitch than this Liverpool team does.'

A common theme in both these matches and, indeed, in rather more games in the 2001–02 season than Liverpool's supporters would care to be reminded of, was the absence of the side's most influential playmaker, the Finn Jari Litmanen. The arrival of Litmanen in January 2001 was heralded by Houllier as his 'most fantastic signing', yet he had great difficulty in integrating Litmanen's talents into his preferred 4-4-2 structure. Although an outstanding footballer, Litmanen lacked pace and tended, when playing as a second striker with Owen, to drop deep searching for the ball in midfield, leaving his partner isolated. The bolder approach would have been to play Litmanen 'in the hole' just off the two strikers in a 4-3-1-2, but this meant Liverpool, who did not have any obvious wingers anyway (with Berger, Smicer and Murphy all preferring to tuck in), became very narrow in their forward play. Houllier's Litmanen dilemma was not dissimilar to the problems experienced by Alex Ferguson in accommodating the £28 million Argentine Juan Veron without upsetting the balance of an already well-established midfield. Initially, Ferguson tried playing Scholes as a second striker – without success – and even relegated Beckham to the bench to allow Veron to operate on the right side of midfield. Later, Cole was sold, Scholes moved to the left and Giggs pushed up alongside Van Nistelrooy.

But Ferguson, unlike Houllier, found it more difficult to switch from the classic 4-4-2. Over the course of the 2001–02 season, Houllier and (in their stricken manager's absence) Phil Thompson rendered criticism of Liverpool's 'negative approach' increasingly redundant by their flexible and, on occasions, daring strategic variations. Houllier's 'bunker' (the successor to the Boot Room, where Houllier, Thompson and French coach Jacques Crevoisier met to formalise match-day tactics and plans) became particularly adept at altering Liverpool's formation not just in a negative way, to stop the opposition playing, but more and more in a manner designed to set their opponents a tactical conundrum they had not been expecting to solve. Against Roma in Houllier's triumphant comeback, Liverpool surprised Fabio Capello by their use of a 4-3-3 formation, with Smicer and Litmanen roaming freely alongside Heskey. Capello had assumed beforehand that, with Liverpool's most potent weapon (Owen) injured, his defence were going to be in for a relatively trouble-free night. He admitted after the Reds' 2–0 victory that he been caught unawares: 'I knew Liverpool were good but I have never seen them play like that.' Had he studied a video of Liverpool's previous home game, against Newcastle, he would have seen a similar attacking configuration in action. Then, the Reds boldly fielded Heskey, Owen and Anelka together in possibly the fastest forward line to ever grace the Premiership and one to send office fantasy football competitors into apoplexy. This use of three strikers, alternating when Liverpool were on the back foot, to a 'Christmas Tree' 4-3-2-1 shape was a positive and imaginative solution to the Litmanen dilemma – not that it necessarily involved playing Litmanen! With only three in midfield, it forced

Liverpool's full-backs to push up in support thereby adding width to the Reds' attacking play.

Danny Murphy's astute footballing brain and much underrated all-round midfield game was a key element in making a success of these tactical switches. Thompson praised Murphy as the most tactically aware midfielder at the club, and the evidence bore him out. After a dip in form that coincided with a collective malaise within the team during Houllier's absence from the dug-out in the 2001–02 campaign, Murphy's resurgence was instrumental to the upswing in performance level that propelled Liverpool to their highest-ever Premiership points tally and the Champions League quarter-finals.

Even when Liverpool chose to employ their favoured 4-4-2, it was never rigidly imposed. Frequently, Liverpool's midfield four played in a diamond shape rather than strung out in a line, with Hamann anchoring, Gerrard wide right, Murphy or Berger on the left and Smicer at the peak of the diamond, linking with the strikers. It was also common for Liverpool's wide midfield players to interchange positions regularly throughout a match. The team's fluidity and renewed attacking vigour during the latter half of the 2001–02 season made a mockery of the criticism that, in particular, accompanied their Champions League campaign. The Spanish newspaper *El Pais* in the build-up to what, almost inevitably, was to be Liverpool's second goalless draw at the Nou Camp in the space of 12 months, wrote: 'A look at the players that have played most in the Liverpool team this season shows the asphyxiating ideological stance adopted by Phil Thompson, whose philosophy can be summed up in the single sentence: "If your two centre-backs are on form, it doesn't matter if the rest of the team is having a nightmare, because you'll manage a draw."' The paper accused Thompson of putting 'another defensive line of four in the area where other teams tend to have midfielders'. This kind of bitter rejoinder was typical of much of the criticism levelled at Liverpool during 2001–02.

Nonetheless, while the emphasis on teamwork, working back to regain possession and closing down space, was essential to Liverpool's success under Houllier, finding the right balance between solidity and creativity often proved elusive, particularly in the early and middle stages of the

2001–02 campaign, when observers were expecting the team to play with a more confident and adventurous spirit after their trophy-winning spree the season before. Houllier had successfully instilled a work ethic into the Reds, but new Liverpool could be laboured (even Jamie Carragher admitted that he would rather watch Arsenal or Manchester United!). Houllier countered criticism that Liverpool were too defensive in their methods and over-reliant on the counter-attack, even at home, by pointing to his side's achievements in that Treble-winning season, stating rather tetchily on more than one occasion that they had done remarkably well to score 127 goals on the counter-attack. And any side featuring some or, occasionally, all of Berger, Owen, Heskey, Gerrard, Litmanen, Smicer and, later, Anelka can hardly be described as lacking flair. Houllier recognised the importance of incorporating individual player brilliance into the mix of progressive team play he preached to his charges, but frequently stressed that his players were still learning and developing – the implication being that, as the side progressed, they would become more assured and forward-thinking in their approach.

Compared, of course, to the great French sides which won the World Cup and European Championship and on whom Houllier's new Liverpool were modelled, the Reds inevitably fell a little short. They lacked the quality forward thrusts, and width, provided from full-back by Lizarazu and Thuram (particularly in Markus Babbel's lengthy absence through illness although John Arne Riise's attacking prowess went some way to compensating for the German's loss) and an outstanding playmaker around which the team's attacking base could be built. Neither Litmanen nor Smicer, good players though they were, could be said to be in Zidane's class. Liverpool's only other visionary passer of the ball in this period, Jamie Redknapp, spent more time on the treatment table than the pitch during Houllier's first four seasons at the club.

Liverpool's new style under Houllier had its casualties, none bigger than Robbie Fowler who, starved of goalscoring opportunities and struggling to regain his old sharpness, became increasingly marginalised under the Frenchman. Fowler had prospered under Evans, not only from playing regularly, but also from Liverpool's constant pressing of the opponent's penalty box and from Evans' use of the 3-5-2 system which allowed the wing-backs (usually McAteer and Bjornebye) to get forward and hit a stream of crosses into the danger area. Fowler suffered under Houllier because he did not thrive on a defensive approach reliant on fast breakaways to create chances. The dramatic 3–2 victory over Everton in the Treble-winning campaign was a classic example of this new approach. Within seconds of Everton appealing for a penalty in the first half, the ball was in the back of their net. Again in the second half, an Everton corner quickly became a Liverpool goal. For this plan of action to work, Houllier needed his fastest men up front to race onto the clearances – and that invariably meant Owen and Heskey.

Fowler had also benefited from Evans' deployment of McManaman in a free role, with licence to roam the pitch in search of attacking opportunities. Houllier never really replaced McManaman, preferring instead to build a team pattern requiring fluidity from all of the midfield players, bar the holding player at the base of the diamond. This meant the other three needed the ability to take it in turns to occupy the 'free' role, to cover for each other and to interchange positions seamlessly several times during the course of a match. When Liverpool were on their game, this system worked brilliantly, as demonstrated in the 2–0 victory over Manchester United in March 2001. The first half was as good a display as any seen under Houllier: Murphy, Berger and Gerrard exposing the gaps between United's suspect defence and midfield with intelligent running into space and purposeful passing. On such a day, Liverpool were unstoppable – who did United man-mark to stem the flow? One moment Gerrard was playing alongside Hamann in a traditional central midfield role; the next whipping in dangerous crosses from the right as Murphy tucked in behind the strikers. Next Berger was linking with Heskey and Fowler and Murphy was wide left, and so on. Under Evans, if McManaman, as the sole creative fulcrum, was man-marked out of the game, Liverpool's attacking options virtually dried up.

When Liverpool were out of sorts, however, particularly during the barren run immediately post-Fowler, the team appeared prosaic, lacking the craft and guile, as well as the width, necessary to break opponents down. The defensive mindset that naturally accompanied the counter-attacking approach often proved difficult to overcome so, for example, if

Liverpool fell a goal behind, it was not easy for the players to adapt their style mid-match to suddenly become more creative and offensive in outlook. It is hard to imagine Liverpool recovering from 3–0 down at half-time to win 5–3 (as Manchester United did in an extraordinary game at Tottenham), or scoring three times in the final fifteen minutes of a match to overturn a two-goal deficit, as United (again!) achieved in the FA Cup against Aston Villa in the same season. (In justification, Liverpool's defence was so much stronger than United's that they rarely needed to score more than one or two goals to win a game.) In fact, Liverpool won only once in the Treble-winning season after falling behind. It was a memorable comeback, however, Michael Owen's double strike sinking Arsenal in the FA Cup final.

Liverpool under Evans pressed forward incessantly. Under Houllier, chiefly in Europe and against their title rivals, they pressed the opposition from the front but in a defensive way designed to prevent their opponents dictating the flow of the game and playing their natural style. This 'pressing defence' tactic was used, with great success, by Arrigo Sacchi during Italy's World Cup campaign of 1994. Sacchi felt such high-pressure tactics developed courage in the players and built up team spirit. It also had the benefit of encouraging the weaker players in the team, as successful execution of the strategy gave everyone a role to play. For the ardent Liverpool historian Houllier, the philosophy that underpinned the pressing game was another way of revitalising the spirit of Bill Shankly within the club – 'Shanks' set great store by working as a team, believing Liverpool's success stemmed from the fact that 'no one was asked to do more than anyone else. We were a team. We shared the ball, we shared the game, we shared the worries.' For Liverpool, the younger players (in particular, Murphy, Carragher, Heskey and Gerrard) all made great strides under Houllier's new system.

Inherent in these pressing defence and counter-attacking strategies was the development of a resolute 'one-for-all, all-for-one' mentality within the side. Houllier deliberately sought to foster this attitude at all times. The new togetherness engendered by the manager was reflected in the Houllier-introduced ritual of the pre-match huddle. Performed by the whole team in the centre circle before the kick-off of each game, it stirred the fans into a frenzy of support at Anfield and provoked derisive whistles and catcalls in away matches. Both responses were, of course, precisely what Houllier was looking for. It was just one more detail in Houllier's tactical masterplan that helped transform Liverpool's fortunes faster (but, conversely, with greater censure) than even the great man himself could have anticipated.

5

Owen and Gerrard: Emergence of the New Generation

Gérard Houllier's Liverpool revolution has been blessed by one of those chance vagaries of nature that all great movements require – a figurehead to inspire, an icon around which to build a philosophy and, in a modern football team, a style that will nurture substance and, with it, success. For Houllier, serendipity struck not once but twice by delivering two once-in-a-generation footballing talents to his front doorstep at precisely the time fate decreed the role Houllier had coveted for years was his for the taking. In the month Gérard Houllier put pen to paper on his Liverpool contract, an 18-year-old star-in-the-making bedazzled a watching world with a spellbinding, electric run through the heart of Argentina's defence, culminating in a nerveless finish that spoke volumes for the character of its perpetrator. The prodigious Michael Owen was England's present and future in one (how could you talk about potential when, at 18, he had already scored a better goal than arguably any Englishman ever to represent his country in the World Cup finals?). And, deliciously, he belonged to Liverpool.

If Gérard Houllier was already positively salivating at the prospect of working with, and developing still further, such a talent, the man whose most recent assignment had seen him guide the up-and-coming stars of French football as coach of the national Under-18s was to unearth a second gem shortly after his arrival on Merseyside. Invited to watch the youth team train, Houllier was so struck by his first sight of another local-born teenager that he transported him straight to Melwood – and the first-team squad. Steven Gerrard, nearly a year younger than Owen despite having been his contemporary during their rise through the ranks at Liverpool, was, whilst a different type of player, as astonishing a prospect as Owen. Houllier, having worked with the young Trézéguet and Henry, among others, knew a special talent when he saw it and, at that moment, Paul Ince's fate as Liverpool's midfield-general was sealed.

As Liverpool lurched from one crisis to another during his first, traumatic season in charge at Anfield, it quickly became clear to Houllier that Gerrard could join Owen as the focal point around which his new team would be built. And although he went on to make several key signings, notably Sami Hyypiä, Dietmar Hamann and Emile Heskey (and later Markus Babbel and Jerzy Dudek), Houllier stayed true to his word in constructing his revamped squad around a Liverpool heart. Owen and Gerrard were that heart and, more so than even the magnificent Hyypiä or the indomitable Hamann, epitomised the youthful, dynamic and richly talented Liverpool of Houllier's vision.

MICHAEL OWEN

Michael Owen was clearly a uniquely gifted footballer long before he set foot on the St Etienne turf one balmy night in the summer of 1998 to rewrite World Cup history. As a 16-year-old representing England schoolboys and Liverpool reserves, he was the subject of several covert bids from leading European clubs during the Euro 1996 tournament staged in England: Owen's name, and goalscoring feats, were already known to football scouts across the continent. Ever since as a 12-year-old boy he had shattered Ian Rush's goalscoring record for Deeside Primary School in North Wales, scoring an incredible 79 goals in one season, Owen had appeared destined for stardom. His exploits brought him an invitation to join the FA School of Excellence at Lilleshall, and once there he continued on his merry way, breaking record after record and displaying an uncanny knack for scoring goals on his debut at each new level he reached: for the England Under-15s, the Under-16s, 17s, 18s and even the Under-21s (whom he represented as a callow 17 year old).

By then, of course, Owen was a fully-fledged member of Liverpool's first-team squad, having risen quickly through the ranks after signing apprentice forms as a schoolboy in 1996 (his first wage was the standard £42.50 a week for YTS apprentices). In the same year he helped Liverpool to victory in the FA Youth Cup, scoring a breathtaking hat trick against his Manchester United counterparts in front of the watching Sir Bobby Charlton. Sir Bobby was beguiled, if not a little disappointed that United's scouts had not snapped him up, recalling: 'I knew he was a special player the first time I laid eyes on him.' Owen finally signed professional terms with Liverpool on his 17th birthday – 14 December 1996. Less than five months later, Roy Evans blooded the teenage sensation in Liverpool's first-team, Owen making his bow as a substitute in the final game of the season at Wimbledon and, inevitably, scoring within moments of his arrival with an assured finish.

Following his first-team debut, Owen spent the first part of his summer representing England in the World Youth Championship in North Africa and the remainder eagerly anticipating his first full season at Anfield as a member of the senior squad. Confident though he was, Owen could not have expected to feature regularly in the first eleven, but a combination of good fortune – Robbie Fowler picking up a pre-season injury that meant he was sidelined until October – and the relish with which he took his opportunity meant that he quickly established himself as a permanent fixture in the team.

By a quirk of scheduling, Liverpool found themselves back at Selhurst Park for the opening day of the new season. Trailing 1–0 with less than ten minutes remaining, Liverpool won a penalty which Owen stroked into the net with ice-cool precision. Did anything faze this 17 year old? Apparently not, as 50,000 partisan Glaswegians could amply testify after watching Owen score with another clinical finish on his first European outing against Celtic, although his strike was ultimately overshadowed by a Steve McManaman wonder goal in the final moments of a vibrant encounter. One landmark which took just a little longer in coming was Owen's first goal in front of his own supporters at Anfield – it eventually arrived against Tottenham on 8 November. By then, the 17-year-old Owen had already been invited by Glenn Hoddle to train at Bisham Abbey with the full England squad, a gesture which, given the rave reviews he was attracting for his club performances, was obviously not meant to be a token one. Although the World Cup was only nine months away, it was not inconceivable that Owen might have an outside chance of making the trip, perhaps as a reserve on standby in the event of injury to a more experienced forward.

While the 1997–98 season was an unremarkable one in the history of Liverpool FC, as the side's form peaked and dipped in its usual parabola of inconsistency, for Michael Owen his first season of professional football was a never-ending fairytale of tumbling records and attention-grabbing headlines. Owen simply took the rule book and ripped it up, discarding, in the process, any preconceived notions of what constituted 'too young' with a series of displays for Liverpool that marked him out as a very special talent. Through all this, Owen emerged as a levelheaded individual who took each jaw-dropping success in his stride. The rest of the country (particularly its teenage female element who, until Owen's emergence, had shown scant interest in football) was won over. The clamour for his inclusion in the full England squad became irresistible and, on 2 February 1998, the Boy Wonder was named in Hoddle's senior England party for the first time. Despite one or two reservations on Hoddle's part (he publicly questioned whether Owen was a 'natural goalscorer' and even issued veiled warnings to Owen and his club regarding the pitfalls of overnight success), Owen became, a week later, the youngest footballer to represent his country in the twentieth century, when he was chosen to start against Chile.

Michael Owen's meteoric rise to the status of a full England international at the age of eighteen years and two months was due to a combination of factors. Raw pace and a deadly eye for goal were his two key attributes, but his abilities went far beyond that. Owen was not merely quick, he was lightning fast, with the acceleration of a top-class sprinter, while his finishing reflected his personality – calm and self-assured. Not for Owen the pumping heart or unsteady aim of a striker confronted by the ultimate psychological test: a one-on-one with the goalkeeper. Owen simply pulled the trigger, as ruthlessly as a seasoned executioner. Beyond these two elements, though, lay something all great sportsmen possess: an innate self-confidence capable of withstanding even the most traumatic lows that are inevitable in any sportsman's career. To this self-belief, Owen added an unbridled enthusiasm for hard work. As the *Daily Telegraph* writer Henry Winter put it, when summing up the respective merits of Owen and Robbie Fowler, 'when not playing through reasons of rotation or injury, Fowler puts on weight while Owen picks up weights'. No sporting great has ever conquered the pinnacle of his game by skill or self-confidence alone.

Whether his ambition realistically extended to representing his country in the 1998 World Cup is another matter. Owen probably had Euro 2000 pencilled in to his schedule as a more attainable goal, but the rapid strides he made through his first year of professional football consigned any such timetable to the drawing board. He finished his first season as the Premiership's top scorer with 18 goals and was now assured of a place in Hoddle's World Cup squad. In England's final warm-up match for France '98 against Morocco, Owen, played through by his club colleague McManaman, scored to break yet another record – that of England's youngest-ever goalscorer. The media began a frenzied campaign for his inclusion in Hoddle's first eleven. Momentum was certainly with the boy from Hawarden, North Wales and, as he gave interviews from England's base camp in the south of France, also the admiration of an increasingly adoring public. One exchange in particular summed up the Michael Owen fairytale. Des Lynam, then anchoring the BBC's World Cup coverage, asked Owen how being involved in a World Cup campaign compared to watching Gascoigne, Lineker and co playing in Italia '90 on television. Owen looked a little puzzled by the question and stated that, as he was only ten at the time of Italia '90, he had very little recollection of it. In that innocently expressed moment, it hit home to Lynam and the viewing public how absurdly young Michael Owen was.

Owen was, however, restricted to a brief appearance as a substitute in England's opening World Cup match against Tunisia, and also failed to start in the next game against Romania. But with England trailing 1–0, Hoddle, the pragmatist coach, finally gave in to Hoddle, the flamboyant player, and uncorked the bubbly: the impact was instant and sensational, Owen scoring a fine equaliser and then running at a panicked Romanian defence to shoot against the post in the dying seconds after an error by Le Saux had given Romania the lead for a second time. England lost, but the impression that a new star had emerged on the world stage was hard to resist. If confirmation was needed, it duly arrived a few days later in St Etienne.

Owen began the game against Argentina having usurped Sheringham as Shearer's strike partner. He ended it playing up front alone, with Shearer reduced to helping out a beleaguered defence, as England, shorn of Beckham (English football's supposed star-in-waiting but, at this point in his career, overshadowed by Owen's more mature attitude) held on for grim life. Owen's electrifying pace tormented Argentina throughout (as it was four years later in the Sapporo Dome in a thrilling reprise of St Etienne): his fearless run into the heart of the South Americans' defence won England's penalty in the opening ten minutes; on several other occasions in the first half he spun past Vivas, or accelerated away from Chamot with ease. He teased Argentina's defenders, luring them into committing fouls, pushing them back in vain to counter his pace. His goal, inevitably, was the defining moment, a devastating combination of nerve, strength, speed and lethal finishing, which left the watching football world awe-struck. 'It was my most important goal, but I scored a better goal when I was playing for England's schoolboys,' Owen mischievously remarked. As he left the field after a night of high drama, one could only pray that Owen would never wise up to how demanding the game can be.

After St Etienne, nothing would ever be the same again for Michael Owen. The first noticeable change was the signing of a new five-year deal at Liverpool on a steeply increased £20,000 a week, amidst rumours that Lazio had offered to pay Liverpool £1.5 million just for the right to have first option on Owen's signature, should he ever leave Anfield. As England visited Sweden at the start of the new season for a Euro 2000 qualifying match, Owen was given a personal bodyguard to protect him from fans who clustered around the hotel where he was due to attend a media briefing. Such was the confusion caused by photographers and TV cameramen clamouring to get close to him, that England captain Alan Shearer was left yards behind, barely noticed. Owen took all this in his stride: 'I've become used to it; it doesn't upset me.' During the trip, which was more akin to latter-day Beatlemania than the visit of an international football team, the Swedish football association revealed they had received hundreds of letters from girls who wanted to be 'ball boys' at the match in order to meet Michael Owen.

Many young players would have found performing to the exalted level Owen had now set himself through his World Cup displays an impossibly tough act to follow. Yet, despite having to cope with a backdrop of soaring public expectation and unremitting media exposure, Owen – with the help and guidance of his new boss, Gérard Houllier – achieved exactly that. The 18-year-old superstar was not about to let fame distract him from the task in hand, firmly stating in the wake of France '98: 'My time has not yet come. I want to keep on scoring goals and stay away from newspaper articles and the media, which will destroy my football.' Although the post-World Cup season was a turbulent one for Liverpool, Owen consistently impressed, again finishing Liverpool's top scorer by some distance, with 23 goals in all competitions despite missing the final month of the season after pulling up with a serious hamstring injury at Leeds. Elland Road represented Michael Owen's first real setback in an otherwise inexorable journey to the top of his profession. It was, as he was to discover over the course of his Liverpool career, the first of many problems with his brittle hamstrings. (Houllier, in one of his more fatalistic moments, likened the recurrence of Owen's hamstring strains to the British weather: you never knew when it was going to rain, but you knew that it would – and when the rain came, there would be nothing that you could do to stop it.) Like Ryan Giggs, another player whose game is based on blistering pace, this type of injury unfortunately comes with the territory. Gérard Houllier was naturally very concerned to ensure his prize investment not only received the best treatment in overcoming his hamstring complaints, but also worked diligently, and proactively, to ensure as far as possible that such injuries were minimised in the future. Liverpool's medical team, led initially by physiotherapist Dave Galley, worked on Owen's posture, particularly his driving position, to build strength in his back. Sparing no expense, Houllier also recommended that Owen visit his friend, the esteemed German consultant Dr Hans Muller Wolfhart, in Munich to seek further assistance in treating his troublesome hamstrings. Dr Wolfhart would soon become well acquainted with Owen and another of Houllier's prodigies, the equally injury-prone Steven Gerrard.

Helping Owen overcome the spectre of recurring injury was but one of several significant contributions made by Gérard Houllier in the furthering of his career. As well as working with him on an individual basis to develop his link-play, team awareness and ability to take opportunities with his left foot, Houllier also provided a culture at Anfield in which Owen could thrive. On the pitch, this manifested itself in the formulation of a strategy geared to maximise his singular talents: the quick counter-attack, feeding Owen's pace with the ball played through early from midfield. Off it, Houllier's determination to bring silverware back to Liverpool meant the instilling of a new discipline which appealed to his dedicated striker. Early in Houllier's reign, Owen spoke appreciatively of the changes wrought at Anfield by the boss: 'I hope that "Spice Boy" thing has gone now. You can see a renewed spirit and a certain steeliness about the team. Although it will take time for everything to gel, there is great confidence that it will.' Owen elaborated: 'We did have a team with a lot of very good players, individuals who would get into a lot of other sides, but we were not getting good enough results for many different reasons. So some players were labelled the Spice Boys. The lads didn't like it, but they've done well to get rid of that tag. It certainly isn't like that at Liverpool any more.'

Houllier's hard work with his star striker on the training ground paid dividends on the pitch to spectacular effect, as Owen, in the space of four months in 2001, used his 'weaker' left foot to score the winning goal in the FA Cup final, the Super Cup and the Charity Shield. In the latter, Owen gave United's centre-back, Jaap Stam, such a chasing that Alex Ferguson decided it was time to move the opinionated Dutchman on to Lazio. Owen's performance at Cardiff also made something of a mockery of Jaap Stam's damning claim (made in his autobiography – another source of irritation for Ferguson) that it was possible to negate Owen's threat simply by showing him onto his left side: 'Opponents have learned to combat (Owen) by dropping off him, ensuring there isn't the space behind them for him to attack. Without that option, he loses much of his potency. I am not saying he is a bad player, but his first touch isn't the greatest. As a defender, you will know a player's particular weakness, and with Owen you try to get him out on his left side.' In the privacy of the dressing-room after the Charity Shield victory, Houllier and Owen would have allowed themselves a quiet smile at Mr Stam's expense.

While Owen quickly established a close bond with his French manager, one particularly interesting aspect of Owen's early Liverpool career was an, at times, cool relationship with the supporters. It is not that the fans did not take to Michael – they were immensely proud of his achievements and appreciative of his contribution to the Liverpool cause – but they did not so easily *warm* to him. It would not be until the 2001–02 season, a full four years after his debut, that Michael Owen's name was heard to be chanted by the Kop. Although he always maintained an unruffled exterior, Owen noticed and remarked to club colleagues on the fact (tellingly, on reaching the milestone of a century of Liverpool goals against West Ham, Owen remarked 'I might not be the most popular player to reach 100 goals'). There were several factors at the root of this odd state of affairs: Owen's manner which, while it elicited admiration, did not so easily inspire passion; the more outwardly emotional Robbie Fowler's pre-eminence as the fans' idol, which pre-dated Owen's emergence and, paradoxically, grew in direct relation to Fowler's growing on- and off-field misdemeanours; and, controversially, the initially often-voiced belief that Owen was somehow an England player first and then a Liverpool player. This latter view was, in part, born out of Owen's superlative feats in the World Cup, which won him universal acclaim, before he had achieved high-profile success with his club. Owen was alone among his Liverpool colleagues in representing England at France '98, save for a brief cameo from McManaman as a substitute. And Steve McManaman's England form remained, Euro '96 apart, consistent only in its inconsistency. He could probably have tried the patience of a Tibetan monk, let alone that of several England managers exasperated by his insouciant performances in the white shirt. With Fowler (whose international career had not taken off anyway) spending the summer of '98 at home recuperating from injury, the focus inevitably fell on Michael Owen.

Perhaps it did not help Owen's cause that he was so openly ambitious about his desire to reach the game's summit, stating on one occasion: 'When I go away with England and I see players like David (Beckham), with a cabinet full of trophies, I think how I'd like to be like that. That is the whole reason I came into the game.' He did however go on to clarify: 'I have no doubt I can achieve that with Liverpool,' but sections of the Liverpool support remained unconvinced, believing the implication to be that Owen would need to leave Anfield for Spain or Italy, or, worse still, Old Trafford to achieve that ambition. For an uncomfortably long time, therefore, a strange contradiction prevailed on Merseyside, where one of the world's greatest football stars, arguably the most important player to represent Liverpool since Dalglish, found it difficult to attain the unreserved affection of the Kop. There was not a great deal Owen could do to alter the fans' misconceptions, short of continuing to give his all for the club, week in and week out – which he invariably did.

It is often argued that the turning point in Owen's relationship with the fans was Fowler's eventual move to Leeds in November 2001, which cleared the way for Owen to be installed as the new 'King of the Kop'. In fact, the thaw began in the previous season. Although he was an unused substitute on the occasion of Liverpool achieving their first trophy under Houllier, and their first in six years (the League Cup), Owen's single-handed destruction of Arsenal to personally hand Houllier the FA Cup on a silver platter brought him the undying love of Liverpool's fans. At last, Owen and silverware were associated in the minds of Liverpool's supporters. He followed that up with a fine contribution to the UEFA Cup victory against Alavés, amidst a glut of goals in the successful push for a Champions League place. Finally, he cemented his standing as a world-class international of the highest calibre with his Munich hat trick against Germany at the beginning of the 2001–02 season, in the process bathing his club in the reflected glory of his triumph. 'Oh, Owen, that was mouthwatering football,' proclaimed one German national newspaper. It was not just that his three goals were lethally taken (a suitably impressed Oliver Kahn described his nemesis as 'cool and clever'), his overall performance demonstrated just how far Owen had come in a remarkably short space of time. Before the match he had spoken of the difference between pace and sharpness. 'I'm a quick footballer, not a sprinter,' he explained. His performance in Munich illustrated his point. A week earlier he had come up against Oliver Kahn in a one-on-one playing for Liverpool in the Super Cup final but had allowed Kahn's bulky frame to block his low shot. When a similar opportunity presented itself at Munich after Gerrard's pass sent him clear, he looked up, steadied himself and lifted the ball over Kahn with precision accuracy. The goal was the product of speed of mind as much as quickness of movement.

By the time, therefore, of Fowler's transfer to Leeds (a move sanctioned, in no small part, by Owen's rise to prominence), Michael Owen had succeeded in winning over the Liverpool fans, as well as establishing himself as one of the finest footballers of his generation. His talents were now widely acknowledged outside his homeland (Pele described him as his 'favourite footballer', Cruyff tipped him to be one of the stars of the 2002 World Cup), a fact recognised by the sport's ultimate accolade: the award of European Footballer of the Year. Beating off the stiffest of competition (Raul, Figo, Shevchenko) to land football's most sought-after honour was a truly special way to round off a memorable 2001 for Owen. He felt 'extremely proud' to have joined such illustrious company: 'Marco van Basten won it three times. Michel Platini as well. I am proud to add my name to those of Franz Beckenbauer, Johann Cruyff, Rivaldo, Bobby Charlton and Kevin Keegan.' At the time of the award, he was still qualified to play for England's Under-21s.

The award of the Ballon d'Or (Owen polled 176 points; Raul with 140 was a distant second) reflected, too, the immense respect in which his peers held him. Coming in the wake of several distasteful episodes involving young English players (Bowyer, Woodgate, Terry, Morris and others), Owen's honour, and the humble way in which he accepted it, also served to reinforce the positive face of English football at a critical time. His coronation as England's first European Footballer of the Year since Kevin Keegan in 1979 (and the first to do so as a Liverpool player, since Keegan's triumphs came during his time with Hamburg), and his right to be spoken of in the same breath as Cruyff, Best, Matthews, Eusebio and di Stefano, was a just reward for Owen's unstinting desire to be the best striker in the world.

While Owen's club career continued to go from strength to strength (fittingly, he marked his final game of 2001 by emerging from the bench at West Ham to drive home his 100th Liverpool goal), his achievements representing England possibly surpassed even his club exploits. By the conclusion of the 2002 World Cup, Owen had played 41 times for his country and scored an impressive 18 goals (from only 32 starts), but it is the timing of those goals and the quality of the opposition that is most revealing. Among the vanquished are Argentina, Germany, France, Brazil (twice), Romania and Denmark, while 13 of his goals have been scored in competitive matches and a further two in his first two games as captain of his country – the first arriving just five minutes into the April 2002 friendly with Paraguay, fittingly enough at Anfield.

Owen's performances in Korea and Japan more than matched his contribution to France '98. He was again England's leading scorer and now has four goals in World Cup finals, the latest addition to his prize collection, a measured strike against Brazil which briefly threatened to take England to the semi-final of the 2002 World Cup. It was not to be, but Owen can look back with satisfaction on a tournament which confirmed his status as one of the world's leading strikers. Even though only three-quarters fit for the Brazil match, Owen still worried Lucio and Roque Junior throughout, as he had the Danish and Argentine defence in earlier matches. After the game, Ronaldo, happily re-established as the world's greatest forward, paid Owen the ultimate compliment: 'If England are well respected, it is because of him. Owen is one of the most talented footballers I know. It's a pleasure to watch him.'

Nonetheless, international football was not always plain sailing for Owen. During Kevin Keegan's incoherent, and mercifully brief, reign as England manager, Owen was subjected to rather peculiar treatment. Displaying a deep misunderstanding of Owen's game, Keegan hauled him off long before the end of each match in Euro 2000, citing his inability to 'hold the ball'. Yet England's performances under Keegan were a return to the dark days of 'Route One', with Adams and Keown pumping long balls up field to a statuesque Shearer and heavily marked Owen. Such prehistoric tactics hardly played to Owen's strengths: his style was not to play as an old-fashioned centre-forward, shielding the ball with his back to goal, but to race onto through passes from a supporting midfield. Keegan made too much of his first touch: it is generally exemplary except when he is low on confidence and trying to move the ball too fast, before he has got it under control. And knowing he was likely to be the first person substituted if things were not working out affected Owen's morale during Euro 2000. After England's early exit from the Championship, Keegan even went so far as to hint that maybe Owen should have a spell representing England at a more junior level. Gérard Houllier quickly warned Keegan that it would be psychologically bad for the player to force him to play for the England Under-21 side. Keegan backtracked but still omitted him from the starting line-up of the prestigious friendly against France. Owen made his point, however, coming on as a late substitute to salvage a draw with a volley of eye-popping athleticism.

Quite why Keegan chose to make the nation's only world-class forward the scapegoat for his team's shortcomings in Euro 2000 has never been clearly resolved. But by singling Owen out for criticism, Keegan unwittingly undermined his own authority: his failure to either utilise his best players or bring out their best after picking them was to prove a significant factor in his downfall. By contrast, his successor, Sven-Goran Eriksson, quickly established a team pattern with which his players were comfortable. Eriksson had no difficulty identifying the core of international calibre footballers around whom to build a team capable of reaching the latter stages of the 2002 World Cup, and Michael Owen and Steven Gerrard were central to those plans.

Owen remains equally essential to Houllier's Liverpool. It was with great delight and no little relief that the Reds were able to announce in September 2001 that Owen had agreed a new four-year deal at the club, tying him to Liverpool until 2005 and raising his salary to, reputedly, between £46,000 and £60,000 per week. The announcement came after protracted negotiations and, while the club were pleased to have secured Owen's signature, the board were privately disappointed that his advisers had refused a five-year extension. Given Owen still had 18 months to run on his current deal, the effect of the new contract was to prolong his commitment to the club by only an additional two and a half years. Liverpool would therefore be in the position of having to renegotiate terms if they wanted to avoid a 'McManaman' as early as 2003. In fact, the former Liverpool star earned himself a public rebuke from Houllier, after offering his opinion on Owen's new contract: 'It was the best he could have done. But I don't think he will fulfil his promise of staying at Liverpool the rest of his career. I think he will leave Anfield just before 2006, when he will be 26, so this may be the last contract he signs for Liverpool. He will have been at the club for eleven years and that is enough to learn his trade.'

Although McManaman was guilty of insensitivity in commenting publicly on an issue as critical to Liverpool's long-term prospects as Owen's future, his reasoning was not without logic. Nonetheless, while the deal did not stand up to close scrutiny, it still represented a huge plus for Liverpool, and reflected well on Owen's loyalty to his boyhood club. Houllier was right to praise Owen's commitment: 'Michael is obviously going to be a key figure for us in the future. He has repeatedly said he wants to stay at Liverpool. The fact that he's put pen to paper demonstrates his belief in what we are building here and the vision we have for the club.' For his part, Owen was quick to acknowledge his support for the cause: 'There has never been a thought in my mind about playing for any other club than Liverpool and I'm obviously delighted to have signed. They have always been incredibly fair by reviewing contracts early and this is one of the many reasons there is such loyalty at Liverpool.'

With Owen's transfer value soaring to a sufficient altitude to have experienced weightlessness following his high-profile destruction of Roma, Bayern Munich, Arsenal, Manchester United and the German national team in the space of nine extraordinary months in 2001, and with big-spending Real Madrid pledging to make Owen their next big-name signing after Zidane, the contract extension was still something of a coup for Liverpool and an indication not just of Owen's loyalty, but of his conviction that with the Reds, he was poised to continue his trophy-winning spree. One could never have imagined McManaman seriously holding the same belief just three years earlier. Then, his courting by Real had always seemed destined to end in his departure from Anfield.

Nonetheless, the feeling remains that it is a question of when – rather than if – Owen will decide to ply his trade abroad. Liverpool finished the 2001–02 campaign empty-handed and, although the improvement under Houllier is evident to Owen, unless Liverpool are able to land one of the big prizes – the Premiership or the Champions League – in the next two seasons, it is conceivable that he will move on. And it may be that to maximise his transfer fee, Liverpool will have to sell him sooner than that.

STEVEN GERRARD

Steven Gerrard is synonymous with Liverpool under Houllier: young, talented, versatile and ambitious, he is the archetypal modern 'box to box' midfielder. Gerrard's abilities mark him out as a truly special player in the Michael Owen class. Think Roy Keane at a comparable age and visualise a player who is more naturally gifted than Keane will ever be, a player who, at just 22, can boast a more accomplished all-round game than Manchester United's captain, if not yet Keane's nous. Gerrard is a sumptuous footballer, an effervescent presence in the heart of Liverpool's midfield, capable of taking a game by the scruff of the neck and stamping his authority on it. Gerrard was born to captain club and country: he should achieve both landmarks within the next five years. The scope of his game is breathtaking: bone-crunching tackles executed with the minimum of fuss, but with the maximum psychological scarring; the vision to play effortless 60-yard passes, switching play in an instant, with unerring accuracy; a killer shot; and an eye for the perfect through-ball or defence-splitting pass. As yet, he lacks only the exquisite first touch and ability to play the game at his own tempo in the manner of the truly great midfielder, a Platini or a Zidane. Nonetheless, Gerrard's rise to star status as Liverpool's key midfielder in a little over two years has been nothing short of staggering.

The Huyton-born Gerrard began his Liverpool career as a YTS trainee attached to the Youth Academy, under Steve Heighway's watchful gaze. When Gérard Houllier took over the reins at Anfield, one of the first things he did was pluck Gerrard from the youth team and begin grooming him for a key role in the engine room of Liverpool's midfield. The 18-year-old Gerrard oozed raw potential, and Houllier wanted him training on a regular basis with the first-team even if, initially, his opportunities to play would be limited. Liverpool's central midfield at the time (Ince and Redknapp) lacked drive and pace and with Houllier already clear in his own mind that the French World Cup-winning side would form the model for his new-look Liverpool, this area (like the defence) needed considerable strengthening. Ince was club captain but his performances had not won the hearts of the supporters. Nor had his inability to exert a controlling influence on the pitch impressed Houllier. So, gradually Gerrard was given a taste of first-team action. He played the full 90 minutes of the second leg UEFA Cup tie against Celta Vigo within a month of Houllier taking sole charge and, displaying admirable versatility, filled in at right-back later in the season in a goalless draw at Elland Road.

Just as Michael Owen grabbed with both hands an opportunity arising from injury to a rival to stake a claim for a regular first-team place, so did Gerrard. Liverpool's reshaped team lined up for the opening game of the 1999–2000 season with Redknapp and Hamann in central midfield but, within 25 minutes, record-signing Hamann had departed with ankle ligament damage. Gerrard's chance for a run in the side had come earlier than either he or Houllier had expected. He rose to the challenge, however, thoroughly vindicating Houllier's decision not to raid the transfer market for a more experienced replacement. Consequently, when Redknapp broke down in training with a serious knee problem almost as soon as Hamann had come back, Gerrard was in pole position to partner the German. It was the start of a blossoming midfield alliance that would serve Liverpool well in coming seasons. Gerrard relished the chance to play a more dynamic role, given Hamann's defensive 'holding' brief. Not that Gerrard was restricted to midfield, popping up as he did at right-back, left-back and even right-wing, and winning rave reviews in all positions. His form was also gaining him friends in high places, most notably England manager Kevin Keegan (who had been impressed by Gerrard's talent, and his cheekiness in 'nutmegging' senior pros at an England get-together that summer). Keegan saw the youthful midfielder turn in a flawless performance against Coventry, playing out of position at right-back, and resolved to include the 19-year-old in his next England squad.

Alas, Gerrard did not make that squad and nor did he join up with the next England training session, nor the next one. In his first full season he found it difficult to get his body to cope with the physical demands of his sport. Houllier was determined to educate Gerrard in the importance of looking after himself and insisted that the teenager was incapable of playing two games in a week while his body continued to grow. Liverpool's medical team quickly got to work on Houllier's midfield prodigy, with Gerrard explaining: 'I do 30 minutes stretching before training and have a warm-down regime I have to carry out after workouts and games.' Nonetheless, Gerrard's various back complaints and groin strains continued to prevent him from winning his first England cap. But his newly found status as English football's rising star had its perks, and even when Gerrard wasn't able to play he was, apparently, still able to perform at peak condition in other areas, as he rather alarmingly confided to one radio reporter: 'I can play anywhere on the park. I'm a bit like that in bed, too.' *Brookside's* Jennifer Ellison was obviously a lucky girl . . .

As well as a suspect back, Steven Gerrard was showing signs of a questionable temperament. In his short career to date, he had been sent off whilst playing for the Under-19s as well as the first-team after a wild lunge in the Merseyside derby. His tackling can be fearsome at times, and, quite deliberately, he will seek, in important matches, to exert his presence on the game early on by making a couple of forceful, but perfectly timed, challenges on key opposition players. The Champions League tie against Roma at Anfield and the pivotal visit to Elland Road, both during the 2001–02 season, are good examples of this. Gerrard has, on occasion, taken things too far and is still prone to a once-a-season sending off and the odd booking, but given his style of play, that is to be expected.

Controlled aggression is very much a part of his game and, from an early stage, Houllier has sought to channel it properly, ensuring that Gerrard remained fiercely competitive but within the bounds of the law. He left his young midfielder out of the side after his sending off against Everton and did not speak to Gerrard for a whole week. Having given the teenager a chance to reflect on the error of his ways, he outlined the need for improved discipline. Gerrard admitted: 'He had a go at me over the sending off and subsequent suspension I picked up against Everton. He told me I needed to be more composed in my play and that he wanted me on the pitch and not the sidelines.' Gerrard learned the hard way, as Houllier made him wait on his return from suspension: 'Didi Hamann came in and I couldn't get back. It was a frustrating time for me. When you have played a little bit, you just want more and more.'

There were also technical flaws in his game which needed ironing out. Under Houllier's expert tutelage, these were addressed and gradually eradicated. 'Steven Gerrard has too much waste in his game at the moment,' explained his boss. 'Sometimes he wants to be decisive too quickly and I will tell him to play a square pass, get the ball back and then play it. As a manager, I have to keep the balance between restraining initiative and encouraging players. But there are areas in which you must not lose the ball in progression, otherwise you are punished for that.' Despite these shortcomings, Gerrard continued to stand out from the crowd. He reminded the Anfield faithful of a young Graeme Souness, while some of the older supporters drew comparisons between Gerrard's explosive style and the venerable Duncan Edwards. Praise came from all quarters, Jan Molby describing Gerrard as 'the most complete British midfielder of all time'. Glenn Hoddle, the man who handed a first England start to Liverpool's other teenage superstar, was equally effusive: 'Gerrard is a terrific talent. He has got good passing ability and he plays with his head up, and that's a rarity nowadays.'

Once he had reclaimed his place in the side, there was no stopping him. With Redknapp's injury ruling him out for the rest of the 1999–2000 season (and, as it transpired, the whole of the following campaign as well), Gerrard wasted no time in forging an impressive midfield partnership with Hamann and, building on the confidence of a sparkling first goal against Sheffield Wednesday, turned in performances of a consistently high standard for the remainder of the year. It was no surprise that Gerrard's first full season climaxed, like Owen's two years previously, with a place in the senior England squad for an international tournament.

Steven Gerrard's 30 minutes of football, as a second-half substitute in England's scrappy 1–0 win over Germany, was the only bright moment in an otherwise undistinguished Euro 2000 campaign. In that brief interlude of crisp, cultured passing and confident tackling, which stood out like a beacon from the dross that surrounded it, England knew they had found a midfielder capable of transferring the swagger and controlled aggression of his club performances onto the international stage. For a second successive tournament, an England campaign had ended prematurely (in the case of Euro 2000, in a state of some disarray), but with a young Liverpool player pointing the way to the promise of a better future.

Like Owen, Gerrard grew in stature in the season which followed his international arrival. The weight of expectation was shrugged aside as he added greater consistency and variety to his game. One of the features of the Treble-winning campaign was his ability to play with authority anywhere Houllier demanded. Often he was used on the right of midfield, at times as an orthodox right-winger. Gerrard's response to being asked to hug the touchline was to demonstrate a hitherto unsuspected aptitude for dribbling past defenders and whipping in dangerous crosses, often (as against Porto and Manchester United) to telling effect. He also added regular goalscoring to his repertoire. Having found the net only once for Liverpool previously, he weighed in with ten goals from midfield, most of them spectacular efforts. The best, undoubtedly, was the devastating 30-yard rocket he unleashed past a startled Fabien Barthez at Anfield. Gerrard crowned the 2000–01 season with a goal in the UEFA Cup final victory over Alavés and the PFA Young Player of the Year award. For good measure, he also pipped Sami Hyypiä to be voted the Liverpool Fans' Player of the Season.

At this juncture in his career, Steven Gerrard is on the verge of being recognised as the complete midfield player. He is not yet as central an influence on the really big games as Keane or Vieira, but that will come with age. Occasionally, too, an impetuous streak will get him into trouble with referees (not that the odd set-to with an official ever held back Keane or Vieira!), while his intuitive desire to play the ball early will sometimes lead to a misplaced pass or two. When Gerrard's confidence was low, during Liverpool's temporary dip in form under Phil Thompson, he seemed to be attempting ever more extravagant cross-field balls to play himself back into form. When they were cut out by the opposition, it looked horrible but Gerrard kept trying to be positive and worked hard to get back his rhythm. He never shirked his responsibility as Liverpool's midfield driving force and his determination saw him through a difficult period. In successive games in 2001–02 against Liverpool's Championship rivals Manchester United, Arsenal and Leeds, he hit sensational through balls to create goals for his team, inspiring those around him to return to the heights that had briefly taken them to the top of the Premiership. That facility for turning matches is one of the attributes that mark Gerrard out as a truly outstanding talent. He has the capacity to exploit space intelligently and decisively, the awareness to read what is going on around him, to make himself permanently available to his colleagues, and the power and energy to be the dominant figure in Liverpool's and England's midfield for years to come.

The only thing that can prevent him fulfilling his undoubted potential is an unfortunate tendency to suffer from injury. Gerrard has struggled throughout his short career with persistent back complaints and, as a consequence, he is prone to suffering groin strains. The back trouble is a legacy of the rapid growth he experienced in his late teens. Gerrard underlined the cause of the problem during the spell in his second full season at Liverpool when he was unable to play two games in quick succession: 'I think it's a mixture of playing so much football between the ages of 14 and 16, coupled with how quickly I have grown in the last few years. Over the last year alone I have grown three inches! When I was 15, me and Michael Owen were the same size.' Like Owen, Gerrard is a regular visitor to French osteopath Philippe Boixel, where he undergoes a programme of manipulation and massage to cure the problem. Nonetheless, with the 2002 World Cup looming and Liverpool entering the final straight of a gripping Championship race, his susceptibility to injury threatened to undermine the ambitions of both club and country. Journalists covering England internationals ritually rely on a cut-and-paste paragraph for their match previews headed 'Gerrard doubtful with groin strain'. True to form, Gerrard departed just 20 minutes into Liverpool's final game of the season (and the day before he was scheduled to meet up with the rest of his England colleagues to begin their World Cup preparations), walking stiffly, but otherwise not unduly inconvenienced. However, the low-key nature of his early exit masked a deeper, underlying problem. Liverpool had been concerned since February that the groin troubles undermining Gerrard's ability to play regularly were not improving, for all the expert treatment he was receiving. Houllier had nursed his star midfielder through the run-in, playing him selectively (and resting him, in fact, for a vital game at Tottenham, which Liverpool subsequently lost). The club broke the news the day after the Ipswich match that Gerrard would not be going to the World Cup – he was instead to undergo an operation as quickly as possible in an attempt to finally cure the problem and to be ready to report back for pre-season training in July. The surgery, similar to that performed on Stéphane Henchoz when he first arrived at Liverpool in the summer of 1999, carried with it a rehabilitation period of six weeks, but the promise, too, of a trouble-free future career (Henchoz has scarcely missed a game in three years). Houllier explained: 'The important thing now is for Steven to have a successful operation so he is available for Liverpool and England next season. It's disappointing for Steven and for me because you want to have your players going to that kind of competition. He would have brought home more experience and more maturity, but Steven will have his chance.'

At 22, time is on Steven Gerrard's side.

6

Hou Let The Reds Out! (2000–01 Season)

What a year! In 12 months, Liverpool – having, over the course of the past decade, spectacularly cornered the market in underachievement – brought no fewer than five trophies back to Anfield and achieved a historic cup Treble unprecedented in British football. In the process, Gérard Houllier's team emerged from the shadows cast by the illustrious Liverpool sides of the '70s and '80s and forged an identity all their own. To the memories of Dalglish, Rush, Keegan, Hansen, Souness and Barnes could now be added the images that encapsulated a season which redefined performance and expectation at Anfield: Gary McAllister, bald head glistening under the Westfalen floodlights, face contorted in ecstasy – the look that said a man-of-the-match performance in a European final was not supposed to happen to a 36 year old, playing out his career in a mid-table footballing backwater; Michael Owen cartwheeling joyously into the shaded corner of the Millennium Stadium, Berger and Fowler rushing to join him in celebrating the last-minute goal that won the FA Cup; Gérard Houllier, drenched in champagne, savouring his first trophy as Liverpool manager; the Kop on the greatest night of European football at Anfield in 20 years, rejoicing in a tumultuous victory over Barcelona; Owen and Babbel ducking as Murphy's free kick bisected them both on its unerring path into the top corner of Manchester United's goal; McAllister's extraordinary 44-yard strike to win a Mersey derby and set Liverpool on an unstoppable drive to glory; half a million lining the streets of Liverpool city centre, decked in red and white, to hail their conquering heroes – just some of the many memories of an unforgettable year.

The 2000–01 season will always be accorded a place among the pantheon of great years in the history of Liverpool FC and, after a decade spent in the footballing wilderness, few Liverpool supporters, on the evidence of the steady but unspectacular progress made in Houllier's first full season in charge, could ever have imagined they would be feasting so soon at such a rich banquet.

The season began in a suitably dramatic style, as Nick Barmby picked his way amongst the broken bottles and barbed wire that figuratively divided Stanley Park in two, to his new home. 'It's not as if he's changed religion or anything,' stated a perplexed Gérard Houllier at the press conference called to unveil Barmby's signing from Everton. This ostensibly naïve remark was a disingenuous attempt by Houllier to play down the furore caused by Barmby becoming the first Evertonian to switch allegiance to the Reds in over 40 years. Liverpool's manager was also kept busy in the early weeks of the season fending off missiles directed at Anfield by Steve Gibson, the furious chairman of Middlesbrough, as Christian Ziege continued his self-imposed exile from the Riverside designed to bring about his move to the Reds. With Ziege holding Boro to ransom and Barmby incurring the wrath of half of Merseyside, the football was forced to take a back seat as the new season opened amid a welter of adverse publicity centred on Houllier's transfer dealings, particularly the allegation that Ziege had been illegally 'tapped up'. According to Steve Gibson and Middlesbrough manager Bryan Robson, Liverpool had behaved improperly by 'discovering' a get-out clause in Ziege's Middlesbrough contract which laid down that an offer of £5.5 million would force Boro to sell, and then promptly offering, you guessed it, £5.5 million for the German's services. Boro called their lawyers in, Ziege shipped himself back to Germany and everyone else wondered how Gibson and Robson could somehow have overlooked that particular part of the contract in the first place. Liverpool got their man, of course, as Boro's bluster amounted to nothing although the case was eventually to come before an FA tribunal over 18 months later, by which time Ziege had long since departed to Tottenham. (Liverpool were fined £20,000 by the FA for their part in the Ziege affair, Gibson's anger exacerbated by Rick Parry's reaction to the fine: 'Doubtless the Premier League is going to busy itself now with dozens of other investigations because this is something that is not unique to Liverpool.' To rub salt into the wounds, Middlesbrough's laughable attempt to sue the Reds for damages was later thrown out by the High Court.)

It didn't take long, however, for events *on* the pitch to claim the headlines, although in an equally unsavoury fashion. Liverpool travelled to Highbury for their opening away fixture and lost 2–0. Shock summer capture Gary McAllister made his debut and, before he could pause to reflect that he was now playing for Liverpool in the twilight of his career, was back in the Highbury changing-room, after being controversially sent off by the referee just 20 minutes into the game. Mr Poll compounded his error by later dispatching Vieira and Hamann, the latter presumably for being tall, German and prone to tackling the opposition. Hamann departed with a rueful smile. It is not often that both sets of supporters are united in condemning the man in black, but Gérard Houllier had it about right: 'The sending off of McAllister was poor. I want the players to be the stars of the game, not the referee. He wrecked it as a spectacle.'

At Highbury, the fans got their first sight of the defensive 4-1-4-1 formation with which Houllier had been experimenting in pre-season. The theory is that by using three central midfielders (forming a triangle, with the holding midfield player operating just in front of the defence), the team would be well equipped to suffocate opposition attacks, while simultaneously using the wide midfielders as added forwards, to support the lone striker. The choice of this formation led, at Arsenal, to the surprise omission of Owen and, with Heskey frequently isolated, it would also prove to be one of the last occasions that the fans got to see it in action (nor did Owen, when fit, spend much more time warming the bench over the course of another prolific season), although the concession of an early goal, McAllister's contentious dismissal and some erratic passing in midfield cannot have helped Houllier make a fair judgement on the tactic's merits. Too often, possession was surrendered cheaply on the halfway line and with novice left-back Traore struggling to cope with the pace of Pires, Liverpool were quickly on the back foot and chasing the game.

Liverpool's early-season form was patchy to say the least. With Fowler again suffering injury problems and Heskey still easing his way into the team pattern, the Reds were reliant on Michael Owen's razor-sharp finishing for those points they were able to muster. There were, however, promising signs that the Heskey–Owen combination was starting to click. In successive home victories against Villa and Manchester City, Heskey made goals for his partner, the strike against City set up by a delightful first-time reverse ball after a masterful piece of chest control. There was clearly more to Heskey's game than pace, power and, John Gregory would probably add, a propensity for falling over.

The defence, however, were not gelling quite as well as in the previous campaign. The arrival of German internationals Markus Babbel and Christian Ziege, together with an injury to Hyypiä, had disrupted the settled system developed by Houllier. Babbel had been close to joining the first wave of Houllier's revolution in the summer of 1999, but Houllier had bided his time to land the versatile Bayern Munich defender on a free transfer 12 months later. It was another shrewd piece of transfer dealing by Houllier and the fact that such a sought-after international should readily swap the Champions League for the less glamorous setting of the UEFA Cup was testimony to how highly thought of the Frenchman was across Europe. Initially, though, Babbel found it difficult to adapt to the frenetic pace of the Premiership and, in particular, to the demands of the right-back role earmarked for him by Houllier, who was reluctant to break up the established Henchoz–Hyypiä centre-back partnership. Meanwhile, Dominic Matteo's transfer to Leeds, to make way for Ziege, meant that Liverpool's back five were now a multinational assortment: a Dutch goalkeeper with a Finn, a Swiss and two Germans competing for places alongside Frenchman Djimi Traore and Liverpudlian Jamie Carragher. Observers wondered whether communication may be a problem. Certainly, none of the defenders appeared to be on the same wavelength at Chelsea, scene of many a capitulation in recent years. On this occasion, Liverpool surpassed themselves, losing 3–0 after a very poor defensive display, characterised by Westerveld punching a corner into his own net inside the first five minutes. Afterwards, Houllier was apoplectic: 'I would have to say that we are a long way from challenging for the title. At the moment we are not at the level of some of the teams in the Premiership like Manchester United and Arsenal. We have to make sure we improve.'

Liverpool's pressurised midfield could have done with new signing Gary

McAllister's experience at Stamford Bridge but, unfortunately, McAllister's Liverpool career to date had been limited to less than 30 minutes' football, his absence caused initially by serving a suspension following his untimely sending off at Highbury and then – more worryingly – by the need to support his wife through the trauma of being diagnosed with breast cancer. After the joy of being handed an unexpected opportunity to play once again at the highest level in the evening of his career by Gérard Houllier, McAllister's delight was obviously tempered by the more pressing concern of his wife's illness. It was a difficult time for the veteran Scot who, happily, was able to return to first-team action for his new club in time for the visit to Derby in mid-October. McAllister immediately brought a greater control to Liverpool's passing and a calm assurance to the frenzied battleground of midfield as the Reds began to find their feet with their best performance of the season to date. Heskey, too, was in commanding form, scoring a fine hat trick and visibly bristling with confidence by the end of the game, which ended in an imposing 4–0 victory that was marred only by Michael Owen suffering serious concussion after knocking his head in the mêlée leading up to Heskey's opening goal.

Heskey continued his excellent form in home wins over Everton and Coventry, rounding off the scoring against the Sky Blues with an adroitly executed lob from the edge of the penalty area to seal a 4–1 victory. Has there ever been a player so capable of transformation by a sudden burst of confidence? Heskey can go from looking like an unwieldy, ineffective journeyman to a world-class international in the space of two games. Fortunately for the Reds, under Houllier's expert guidance, it was more often the latter. The opening goal against Coventry had been scored by another of Houllier's well-judged signings – Gary McAllister, who was revelling in the role of elder statesman in midfield, tutor to the prodigious Steven Gerrard. After McAllister's first goal for his new club, Houllier could not resist a little dig at the critics who had expressed their surprise at his decision to sign the Scot: 'I am pleased to hear some people call him a bargain now because I heard so many funny stories when I bought him!' Barmby, too, got in on the act of scoring against a former club in the Mersey derby, an already fractious event given an added edge by his presence.

Liverpool's form, however, remained inconsistent and, after defeats at Tottenham and Newcastle, the Reds went into a home game with Ipswich needing three points to stay in touch with the leading group. Houllier, mindful of upcoming matches with Manchester United and Arsenal, decided to rest Heskey for the visit of the East Anglians, preferring to pair Owen and Fowler from the start, for only the second time all season. The move backfired, however, as Liverpool slumped to a demoralising defeat. Oddly, Houllier came in for fierce criticism for leaving out the in-form Emile Heskey (were these the same critics who campaigned for Fowler's inclusion alongside Owen week after week?). Rather more predictably, he remained unrepentant: 'I'd do exactly the same again. The season is a long one and Emile has played in a lot of hard games; if he plays every game he will end up drained.' Marcus Stewart admitted that the Ipswich players could not believe their luck when they realised that Heskey was not in the line-up. 'The lads were delighted when we realised he wasn't in – we were going round saying, Heskey's not playing! Heskey's not playing! It meant we changed our game plan and we all felt that it gave us a chance.'

A week shy of Christmas and Liverpool's season had reached a crossroads. To talk in terms of a crisis would be to overstate the team's problems, particularly given their good run in Europe thus far, but with Manchester United and Arsenal the next two hurdles to overcome and with six defeats suffered in their first 17 games, it is fair to say that Houllier's men were treading water, and the prospect of Liverpool qualifying for the Champions League appeared as unlikely as Steve McManaman admitting he took creatine. Moreover, Liverpool's record in recent years against United made for particularly distressing reading: no wins in the past 12 meetings, no victory at Old Trafford in the history of the Premiership. But on Sunday, 17 December 2000, Liverpool finally overcame the psychological hold that Alex Ferguson's team had held unchecked for years over the Merseysiders with an assured and disciplined display, running out 1–0 victors. The decisive goal, while a moment of high drama, arrived by virtue of an act of inexplicable stupidity. Gary Neville, for reasons known only to him, decided to indulge in a spot of volleyball on the edge of his penalty area and Murphy curled the resultant free kick round the wall and into the top corner of United's net. Thereafter, Liverpool duly repelled wave after wave of United attacks with surprising ease, new Croatian signing Igor Biscan striking up an instant rapport with Gerrard in midfield and, time and again, sticking out a telescopic limb to emerge triumphant from a tangle with Keane or Scholes with the ball. The lugubrious Biscan may have appeared to be carrying the weight of the world on his shoulders, but his lithe 6' 4" frame, alongside the equally wiry Gerrard, gave Liverpool an athletic, dynamic central midfield pairing more than capable of holding their own with United's more renowned pair. Houllier's stifling tactics also played a significant role in the victory and, in fact, had Liverpool made better use of their counter-attacking opportunities they would have won with far greater comfort. Nonetheless, Gérard Houllier was understandably delighted with the 1–0 scoreline: 'United were the only team I had never won against, so now it's done. I'm pleased for the team, for the players and for the fans. Not many Liverpool teams have won here so I'm really proud of them. It was a great performance. To beat Manchester United at Old Trafford is something special.'

Liverpool followed the Old Trafford coup by beating fellow Champions League rivals Arsenal 4–0 on a bitterly cold Saturday a couple of days before Christmas. While the scoreline ultimately flattered the Reds, the manner of the performance, particularly in the second half, was encouraging. Gerrard and Biscan again competed magnificently in the central midfield tussle against the mighty Vieira, and Heskey's physical presence, allied to his fine hold-up play and awareness of his colleagues, gave Arsenal's defenders a torrid afternoon. The undoubted star of Liverpool's eyebrow-raising victory, however, was Steven Gerrard. It was fast becoming noticeable that, in Gerrard, Liverpool had unearthed a rare talent. To compete with Keane and Vieira (arguably the two best all-round midfielders in the Premiership) in successive weeks and, on both occasions, to come out on top, was a remarkable feat. For Gerrard to reach such heights as a 20 year old, playing in only his second full season, was staggering.

The other pleasing aspect of Liverpool's victory was the cameo played by the perennially out-of-sorts Robbie Fowler. After an indifferent start to the season, caused in the main by a lengthy lay-off through injury and a subsequent relegation to the bench by the fine form of Emile Heskey, Fowler's Liverpool future appeared more clouded than overhead conditions at Headingley on the first morning of a Test Match. Against this backdrop of unrest, Chelsea's new manager, Claudio Ranieri, felt emboldened to approach the Liverpool board with a firm £12 million offer for Fowler's services. The board gave their approval to the move. Houllier, still juggling the perplexing Owen–Heskey–Fowler equation, was categorical: Fowler was going nowhere (at least for the time being). He duly took up his place on the substitutes' bench for the visit of Arsenal. With the Reds three goals up and cruising, Fowler was finally unleashed on his favourite prey. Predictably, he scored, nonchalantly teasing the ball into the far corner of the goal after Barmby played him through Arsenal's weary defence in the final minute of the match. He turned and smiled, almost apologetically, to Houllier as the Kop bayed their approval.

Nonetheless, the gloss was taken off Liverpool's resounding triumph against the Gunners by the 'Fowler to Chelsea' rumours. As the speculation mounted, Houllier was at pains to emphasise that Robbie's future lay at Anfield. 'Chelsea have already revealed their interest and we have had enquiries from two or three clubs recently. But we have told them all the same – Robbie is not for sale. I don't want him to leave. I have spoken to my board and I have made it clear I do not want to lose Robbie. He is part of my plans and very much part of the future. I have always been behind him and I will remain behind him. Hardly anywhere is there a player with his scoring instincts. What we need is for him to reach his level, but I know he can do that.'

Alas, the Fowler stories – like Liverpool's notoriously erratic form – were not about to disappear just yet. After a Boxing Day defeat at Middlesbrough which left Houllier seething at Venables' tactics in a manner which recalled the old adage about glasshouses and stones ('they played like an Italian team with eleven men behind the ball. Today it is more like lucky Venables than Terry Venables. I am still stunned by this defeat'), Liverpool began the New Year on familiar ground, in the midst of a tabloid feeding frenzy on the subject of Robbie Fowler. The latest mishap to befall the unfortunate striker was a punch-up that took place at two o'clock in the morning outside Liverpool's Wonder Bar in Slater Street. While Fowler was the victim of an unprovoked assault, his presence in the heart of Liverpool's clubland in the early hours of the morning angered Houllier. Given that Fowler was still

ABOVE: Steven Gerrard fires home a 30-yard rocket against
Manchester United in the Treble season's 2–0 victory.

BELOW: Owen latches onto Smicer's pass to put Liverpool ahead
against Barcelona in the Champions League.

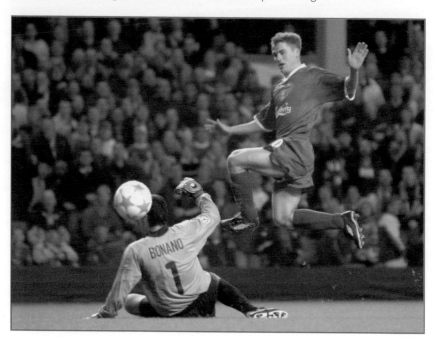

An emotional Gérard Houllier returns to the fray for the visit of Roma – his first appearance at Anfield in more than five months.

ABOVE: Patrik Berger unleashes a trademark left-foot drive on the Arsenal goal as Liverpool search vainly for an equaliser in last season's critical summit meeting. The Reds' failure to break down ten-man Arsenal had a significant bearing on the title race.

LEFT: Michael Owen celebrates the opening goal in Liverpool's 3–1 victory over Manchester United in the first league game to be played at Anfield since Houllier was admitted to Broadgreen Hospital suffering from chest pains on 13 October 2001.

ABOVE: The Kop's tribute to Liverpool's
stricken manager before the same game.

BELOW: Danny Murphy weaves his way through Newcastle's defence en route
to scoring his second and Liverpool's third goal in a 3–0 win over title rivals
Newcastle. Smicer, who has just flicked the ball into Murphy's path, looks
on. Murphy and Smicer both suffered more than their fair share of criticism
during the 2001–02 campaign.

Robbie Fowler shoots at goal for the last time as a Liverpool player. Moments later Hamann was sent-off and Fowler sacrificed in the tactical readjustment. He did not re-emerge for the second half as Liverpool held firm to register the 1–0 win over Sunderland that took them to the top of the Premiership. By the end of the week Fowler was a Leeds player.

Gamekeeper turned poacher: Sami Hyypiä, Liverpool's new club captain
following Jamie Redknapp's departure, shows his delight after scoring
the winning goal in the first leg of the Champions League quarter-final
against Bayer Leverkusen. Steven Gerrard and Emile Heskey join the celebration.

Jari Litmanen wheels away after scoring against Arsenal. Litmanen's vision and touch have made him a popular figure during his time on Merseyside, but Gérard Houllier has not always found it easy to integrate him into his preferred 4–4–2 formation.

ABOVE: Owen and Heskey in tandem – Houllier, like Sven-Goran Eriksson, sees Heskey as the perfect foil for Owen and the success of their partnership has kept first Fowler and then Litmanen and Baros on the sidelines.

BELOW: John Arne Riise: how did you score that goal? It appears that he isn't sure himself – every free-kick since has gone into the wall or the stands. Can someone else assume the responsibilty next season please. Danny? Paddy? Anyone?!

struggling to regain full fitness and, with it, a place in Houllier's first eleven, this latest episode did nothing to assuage the doubters' view that Fowler's long-term interests would be better suited by a move away from his native Merseyside. Houllier's patience was understandably beginning to wear thin and when, a couple of days later, he announced the capture on a free transfer from Barcelona of Jari Litmanen, it appeared that Fowler's days at Anfield were numbered. As the 2000–01 season unfolded, however, Fowler was to play an increasingly ubiquitous role in his side's divergent trophy challenge.

First, however, it was Litmanen's opportunity to take centre-stage, albeit briefly, and the luxuriantly coiffured Finn (okay, it was close to a mullet) wasted no time in adding his own particular blend of silky skills, penetrative passing and all-round awareness to the Liverpool attack. On his league debut against Aston Villa, Litmanen was instrumental in almost all the Reds' best moments, linking intuitively with Murphy and Gerrard as the latter drove in the second of three fine goals. The Villa game was noteworthy, too, for a distinguished contribution from Dietmar Hamann in the holding midfield role. Hamann's form in the current campaign had not been all it might have and the German was starting to come in for stick from supporters expecting more from an £8 million international. Against Villa, Hamann, having wrestled back his place from Biscan, really imposed himself, working tirelessly to protect the back four and using the ball incisively rather than, as had latterly been the case, holding it for too long and being caught in possession. Hamann's return to form was confirmed in the monumental victory against Roma in the Stadio Olympico a month later, when his calm and authoritative display was the pivotal reason for Liverpool restricting the *Serie A* leaders to scarcely a shot on Westerveld's goal.

Before then, Liverpool had reached their first cup final in five years, courtesy of a thrilling 5–0 win over Crystal Palace in the League Cup semi-final and had defeated Leeds at Elland Road to keep alive their FA Cup aspirations. The Palace encounter was presaged by some rather foolish remarks by Palace's young striker, Clinton Morrison, who chose to publicly offer Michael Owen the benefit of his advice on the art of finishing after Owen had uncharacteristically missed several clear chances in the first leg.

Morrison would have been better advised to keep his own counsel; Liverpool tore into Palace from the off in the return at Anfield and quickly put the tie beyond doubt with three goals in the first 20 minutes. Morrison exacerbated his misery by kicking fresh air when the ball landed invitingly for him in front of the Liverpool goal, leading Gérard Houllier to note acidly: 'When you spit in the air it can sometimes land in your face.'

The confidence engendered by defeating Roma so comprehensively in their own stadium propelled the Reds past Manchester City and on, into the quarter-finals of the FA Cup. Smicer and Litmanen were the stars of the show as City were swept away on a tide of pacy counter-attacking football, played as Houllier wanted it – with purposeful passing and terrific movement off the ball. In that mood, First Division Birmingham City should have proved eminently beatable in the first Cup final to be hosted at Cardiff's spectacular Millennium Stadium. That it did not turn out that way was due in no small part to nerves, and an unnecessarily cautious approach, creeping into Liverpool's play after Fowler had given them an early lead with a strike that was as instinctive as it was breathtaking. Sensing that Liverpool were unwilling or unable to build on their lead, Birmingham gradually started to push the Reds back and assert their authority on the game. Their cause was helped greatly by Gerrard departing midway through the second half with cramp. Birmingham renewed their assault on Liverpool's goal and, dramatically, won – and converted – a penalty in the final minute of normal time. Liverpool, who had been so close to giving Gérard Houllier his first trophy, were shaken and for the first period of extra-time could barely string a couple of passes together as they struggled to find the mental resolve to battle through having to effectively go out and win all over again. Birmingham were plainly the fresher team and clearly believed Liverpool were there for the taking. However, after one heart-stopping moment as Henchoz appeared to dive in to a tackle in the penalty area, Liverpool held their nerve and summoned up the deepest reserves of character and determination instilled in them by two and a half years of Houllier's tuition. The side's Teutonic backbone, Dietmar Hamann and Markus Babbel, came into their own as other nationalities wilted, Hamann striking the post with a 25-yard drive and Babbel tearing up and down the right flank, urging his team mates forward. After a tense penalty shoot-out had handed Houllier that all-important first trophy, he paid tribute to the resilience of his side and, in particular, his German stars: 'My English players had gone down. The ones who really put us in charge again were the Germans. They looked tired but still went forward, still went on doing their job. I think you need character in England. You can't have softies.'

There was no time for Liverpool to enjoy the League Cup triumph, however, as the ongoing Premiership, UEFA and FA Cup campaigns all presented an even bigger challenge for Gérard Houllier's men. The League Cup success was a notable achievement, but given the tournament's relatively low-key status its importance lay, as Houllier realised, primarily in the psychological impact it would have on the players. Success breeds success and beating Birmingham after a gruelling, energy-sapping 120 minutes gave the team the confidence to know it could emerge from the toughest of assignments as winners.

That mental strength was very much to the fore as Liverpool continued their impressive progress in the UEFA Cup, first surviving an incessant battering by Roma in the return leg of their fourth-round tie at Anfield by the slimmest of margins, thanks to a resolute defensive display masterminded by the indomitable Hamann, and then engineering a dull but solid 0–0 draw in Porto. The Roma game was notable for an eccentric refereeing display from the Spanish official, Jose Garcia-Aranda. Late in the second half, with Roma trailing 2–1 on aggregate and Michael Owen having already missed a penalty, the ball was crossed into Liverpool's penalty area where it clearly struck Markus Babbel on the arm before deflecting behind the goal. The Kop held its breath as Garcia-Aranda immediately pointed to the spot and then, to general amazement within the stadium, not least its Italian contingent, changed his mind and gave the visitors a corner. In the ensuing fracas, any number of Roma players could have been booked as the referee was surrounded and jostled. As tempers frayed, the game ended with Liverpool holding on for dear life to their slender advantage amidst Roma players flying into vicious tackles and Tommasi receiving his marching orders after pushing Fowler in the throat. At the conclusion of a night dedicated to the memory of Bob Paisley, which, thanks to the Kop's full-bodied support, brought back vivid memories of Liverpool's glorious past, Houllier, never one to make a banquet out of a snack, however tasty, was a relieved man: 'Roma are a tremendous side and better than us at the moment, and we are very happy to be through because we have beaten a very important team in Europe.'

Liverpool's place in the semi-final of the UEFA Cup was duly booked by a comfortable 2–0 win against Porto at Anfield. Michael Owen, who had shaken off a succession of injuries and a spell of indifferent form either side of Christmas, proved the inspiration with a series of exhilarating runs into the Porto defence that recalled vintage Owen circa '98. In fact, Michael Owen was rapidly developing into the complete striker under Houllier's expert tutelage, adding a greater all-round awareness to his game and demonstrating, through his relentless quest for perfection, a newly acquired ability to finish with his left foot and head. Perhaps the enforced mid-season break had served Michael well. He was hungry to play his part in Liverpool's all-conquering season and buoyed by his double strike in Rome, oozing confidence as the campaign entered its final phase.

Not that Liverpool needed him to beat the runaway leaders, Manchester United, 2–0 at Anfield at the end of March. With Owen rested ahead of the trip to the Nou Camp to take on Barcelona later in the week, Heskey and Fowler started up front against United with Berger making a surprise, though welcome, return after the best part of six months out recovering from knee ligament damage. Liverpool produced their best 45 minutes of football all season in the first half against United, time and again scything through the visitors' defence with some sublime passing and fluid interchanging of positions. The central figure in all this was the towering Steven Gerrard who had grown in stature through the 2000–01 campaign to the point where not only was he now considered indispensable to England, he was even attracting envious glances from Alex Ferguson, who cursed Liverpool for unearthing such a gem of a player in the mould of their own Roy Keane. For Keane was eclipsed as Gerrard set Liverpool on their way with an outrageous 30-yard bullet of a shot that was arguably the best goal seen at Anfield in years. His delicate chip played in Fowler for a typically elegant finish for the second and had Heskey and Berger taken their chances, Liverpool could have been four or five goals up at the interval. They took their foot off the gas in the second period and consolidated after Murphy was sent off for an impetuous challenge, but United rarely looked like scoring.

Nobody looked like scoring or, for that matter, shooting at the opponents' goal a few days later as Liverpool and Barcelona played out an infamously turgid goalless draw in front of 100,000 aghast Catalonians. Houllier made no apologies for his team's defensive tactics, and nor should he have done. What chance would Liverpool have had of qualifying for the UEFA Cup final if they had been faced with having to overcome a three- or four-goal deficit in the return leg? Manchester United, Leeds and Chelsea had all perished by similar margins at the Nou Camp in recent years, but Liverpool were too canny, too well-organised and too strong defensively to suffer a similar fate. In fact, theirs was a display of defensive *catenaccio* par excellence. After a few early-season wobbles, Liverpool's back four had been in commanding form, and no matter how frequently Houllier rotated midfielders or strikers, Babbel, Hyypiä, Henchoz and Carragher were, for opposition forwards, a demoralising constant in Houllier's team selections.

The fixtures were now coming thick and fast, consequently exacting punishing demands on Houllier's men. Before Liverpool entertained Barcelona in the return leg, there was the small matter of a key encounter with Champions League rivals Leeds and the Merseyside derby to contend with. Gérard Houllier felt his team were being stretched to the limit and complained bitterly at the rescheduling of a game at Ipswich just three days prior to the Champions League showdown against Leeds. In fairness, the Premier League were hard pushed to squeeze another fixture into Liverpool's overcrowded calender – the Reds were simply a victim of their own success. Leeds came to Anfield and duly won, 2–1. The Champions League now looked out of reach for another season and, to add to Houllier's woes, Steven Gerrard was facing a suspension after letting his impetuosity get the better of him and, as a result, being sent off for clashing with Batty. 'There was bound to be a payback, and we got it against Leeds,' said Houllier. 'That was a vital match for us, but we just weren't there. We bounced back against Everton on Easter Monday, but if you'd asked me I'd have said I would have preferred to lose the Merseyside derby and win against Leeds.'

With less than a minute remaining of the Easter Monday clash at Goodison Park, Liverpool's season was teetering on the brink. Vanquished by Leeds three days earlier, and having seen Everton fight back twice to equalise while Fowler missed the penalty that would have put his team 3–1 up, Liverpool – down to ten men with Biscan the latest red card victim – were exhausted and resigned to dropping two more points. What energy or spirit could they possibly summon when they met Barcelona in just three days' time – their sixth critical game in just 14 days? A draw was not enough for their Champions League aspirations. Leeds, buoyed by their Anfield victory, were threatening to disappear out of sight and the Reds could not afford to drop any more points, least of all at relegation-haunted Everton. As the derby moved into its 94th minute, the young Liverpool substitute, Gregory Vignal, began a determined run from deep within his own terrain and, half falling, half tripped by an Everton defender, won a free kick in a manner which called to mind Paul Gascoigne's surging run in the last minute against Belgium in Italia '90. Vignal, like Gascoigne, seemed to be awarded the kick more out of sympathy for having embarked on such a momentous journey into opposition territory only to be thwarted at the last, than for any wrongdoing on the part of the defender. The decision didn't really bear close scrutiny, but bearing in mind the consequences of Gascoigne's free kick the omens were good. As the entire Liverpool team, bar Westerveld, took up their positions in the Everton penalty area ready for one last, desperate assault on Everton's goal, McAllister shaped to curl the kick to the far corner of the box. Moments earlier a free kick from a similar situation – around 40 yards out – had been met by a soaring header by Hyypiä, only to be brilliantly saved by Paul Gerrard in the Everton goal. Now, Gerrard started inching slowly across his goalline towards the far post ready to deal with the next challenge. McAllister played along, raising his arm and glancing ostentatiously toward Hyypiä and the crowd that had formed at the far edge of Everton's penalty area. To a backdrop of shrill whistling from the home supporters frantic for the end of the game, McAllister stepped forward and, with Gerrard moving to his left in anticipation of a cross, flighted the ball in an exquisite, deadly accurate arc into the bottom right-hand corner of the goal from fully 44 yards. As the net bulged, McAllister sprinted ecstatically to the far touchline to be mobbed by the Liverpool substitutes and, hot on their heels, his team mates. Gérard Houllier, arms outstretched before him in disbelief, wore the look of man in a state of epiphany. There was no time even for Everton to restart the game – the final whistle barely interrupted Liverpool's joyful, cavorting celebrations. An elated Gary McAllister bathed in the glory of his moment of inspiration: 'A point here was of no use to us whatsoever. I've scored a few free kicks down the years but that one has to be one of the best. It was more about disguise than power and pace.'

If ever one extraordinary kick of a football can change a season, it was McAllister's absurdly unlikely shot that redefined the meaning of the word 'speculative'. In that single moment, Liverpool rediscovered the belief and confidence that was to carry them through the demanding final straight of their marathon campaign, borne along by the conviction that this was to be their year. Old Baldy himself, Gary Mac, played like a man reborn, his 36-year-old frame covering every blade of grass with the zest of youth. Inspired by his wonder goal, McAllister's influence grew to a disproportionate level in a team of young bucks, easing alongside Gerrard and Hamann in the engine-room of Liverpool's midfield, conjuring vital goals at key moments, prising open opposition defences with slide-rule passes and, through all this, somehow managing to merge the experience of nearly 20 years of top-flight football with the exuberance of his younger, Championship-winning self. Not that McAllister had a monopoly on dramatic last-minute winners: Liverpool became rather adept at pulling rabbits from the hat in the breathless finale to the season. But McAllister's 44-yard strike was perhaps the most significant of all, presaging as it did an astonishing run of nine wins and one draw from Liverpool's final ten games.

That sequence began in the pressure-cooker atmosphere of Liverpool's biggest European match since Heysel. Their opponents, Barcelona, were patently the better team and were hell-bent on redressing the balance of the Nou Camp stalemate but, urged on by a passionate and vociferous crowd, Liverpool carved open Barça's defence several times in an exhilarating first half, as the tie continued to lie, goalless, in the balance. Then, as half-time approached, Kluivert inexplicably handled a corner and McAllister (who else?) stepped up to fire the resultant penalty into Reina's goal. The second half was nerve-racking but, inspired by a magnificent defensive rearguard action, co-ordinated by Henchoz and Hyypiä, Liverpool held firm to reach their first European final in 16 years.

From there it was relatively plain sailing until the final, tumultuous week of the season. A succession of opponents were brushed aside with ruthless efficiency as Liverpool moved through the gears. Only Chelsea were able to prevent the Reds from claiming yet another scalp en route to the Treble, as Hasselbaink twice cancelled out Owen's predatory strikes in a game that served as a canvas for two supreme talents to display their enviable striking prowess. Owen was in the middle of a hot streak – after six weeks without a goal he had now scored six in his last three matches, including a clinically taken hat trick against Newcastle that had the venerable Bobby Robson enthusing over the boy's singular ability to destroy even the best defence. Nor was he yet finished for the season.

Liverpool entered the climax of their campaign, the now-fabled week of 'three Cup finals': Arsenal at the Millennium Stadium in Cardiff in the FA Cup, Alavés in Dortmund for the UEFA Cup and Charlton at the Valley in the final league game of the season, a 'must win' if Liverpool were to ensure qualification for the Champions League and by default, therefore, a cup final in itself and, arguably, the most important game of the three, financially at least. Three games in eight days that would test Liverpool's mettle to the utmost and provide them with the opportunity to make history as the first English team to ever win a triumvirate of cups in one season. No one dared believe that the impossible could become reality – that Liverpool could emerge triumphant from all three matches – but the doubters reckoned without the unbowing spirit and resilience of Houllier's reborn side. Their mental toughness, together with a superb tactical discipline and defensive capacity of the highest order, had seen them through many battles already in their demanding journey thus far: overcoming Leeds and Chelsea in the domestic cup competitions, twice victors over the newly crowned League Champions Manchester United in the Premiership and, most impressive of all, able to boast an unbeaten away record in Europe stretching through the season, despite being drawn to play against Rapid Bucharest, Barcelona, Roma, Porto and Olympiakos. Liverpool were ready for the ultimate challenge.

On paper, Arsenal looked the toughest of the three assignments, boasting the peerless attacking skills of Henry, Pires and Ljungberg ahead of the midfield-general supreme, Patrick Vieira. And so it was to prove, although initially it was Liverpool's team selection that was the greater source of intrigue. All eyes centred inevitably on one man: Robbie Fowler. Owen, of course, was assured a starting place, but with Heskey out of form (notwithstanding his five goals in the FA Cup run) and Litmanen still feeling his way back after suffering a broken bone in his wrist playing for Finland against England at, of all places, Anfield, the second striking position was up for grabs. However, Fowler (like McAllister) was omitted and could not hide his disappointment as he disembarked from the coach on arrival at the Millennium Stadium, while Heskey started up front and Smicer joined Hamann, Gerrard and Murphy in midfield. Houllier, like his opposite number Arsène Wenger (who left Bergkamp on the bench), was not a man to be guided by sentiment. In the first final to be played in Wales and the first to feature two foreign managers, Liverpool emerged out of the tunnel into the dazzling May sunshine sober-suited, grey in contrast to their last, cream-suited appearance in 1996. No matter what the result, Liverpool weren't going to embarrass themselves in the fashion stakes this time around.

Liverpool started brightly in the searing heat, but Vieira quickly imposed himself in midfield and Arsenal could count themselves unlucky not to be a goal ahead at half-time, after Ljungberg played Henry clear and the Frenchman took the ball round Westerveld, only to see his goal-bound shot deflected past the near post by the falling Henchoz's arm. It was a clear-cut penalty, and Liverpool continued to ride their luck in a far more eventful second period as the heat took its toll and the game started to open up. As the game reached boiling point, Hyypiä, twice in a matter of minutes, dramatically cleared shots off the goalline, first from Cole, then Ljungberg, as Arsenal pressed forward incessantly. McAllister was introduced to the action, replacing the subdued Hamann, as Houllier attempted to bridge the gap between the withdrawn midfield and isolated attackers, but with Smicer a peripheral figure and Gerrard unable to match the more experienced Vieira in the heat of battle, the change did not bring about any immediate dividend. In fact, Arsenal finally took a deserved lead on 71 minutes, as the increasingly influential Pires slipped Ljungberg through to glide past Westerveld and score. Within moments, Henry wasted a gilt-edged chance to put Arsenal out of sight, Hyypiä making another last-ditch block in front of his goal after Henchoz, leading a charmed life, had again handled in the area after slipping. It proved to be the turning point. With a quarter of an hour remaining, Houllier brought Fowler and Berger into the fray, as Liverpool at last abandoned their stifling tactics and started to attack in numbers for the first time in the match. Arsenal got a foretaste of what was to come as a clever pass by Gerrard with the outside of his foot played Owen through, but Keown smothered the danger. Next, McAllister swung over a free kick, the ball was headed back across the penalty area by Babbel, and Owen, reacting sharply, jackknifed his body to volley athletically into the far corner of the goal. 'I was pleased with the goal,' Owen remarked afterwards, 'it reminded me of the one against Romania in the World Cup.'

The game had suddenly shifted towards Liverpool, as the confidence engendered by the equaliser spread through the team. Berger's introduction, as a natural left-footer on the left of midfield, had given Liverpool a better balance, and it was the Czech's coruscating long pass that set Owen clear for the winning goal. And what a goal. Although Berger's delivery was weighted perfectly, Owen still had to deal with Dixon and Adams. Dixon, in fact, was favourite to win the race to the ball, but Owen left the veteran trailing in his wake and, despite being forced onto his weaker left foot, took the ball early, shooting emphatically across Seaman into the far corner of the net. It was a fantastic strike, and one that very few forwards in world football would have been capable of. The unrestrained joy of Michael Owen's celebration, as he cartwheeled towards Liverpool's supporters, was something to behold. Scoring the winning goal in the FA Cup final was another boyhood dream fulfilled, but one of special significance for Owen, who cherished the double strike that had single-handedly won the cup for Liverpool: 'I will go to bed every night dreaming about those goals. It was better than scoring in the World Cup.' Owen's incredible finishing had been like two nails driven deep into Arsenal's heart. They were not so much defeated as emotionally eviscerated by the end of an exhausting 90 minutes. Gérard Houllier, shirt sleeves rolled up, mopping sweat from his brow, beamed ecstatically as he reflected on a wonderful result: 'We were up against a team that is better than us in some areas but in Cup finals anything can happen. I liked my team's performance and I never thought we were out of the match. The will to win is as important as the skill to win and we never let our heads drop.' Jamie Redknapp, in his shirt and tie (does he still own a football kit?), held the cup aloft alongside Hyypiä and Fowler, and Liverpool milked the applause of the Millennium Stadium, which had proved a worthy venue for England's showpiece final. As the players and coaching staff celebrated in front of their fans, singing along to a communal rendition of 'You'll Never Walk Alone', it was impossible to escape the impression that Liverpool were on the verge of reclaiming their place at the pinnacle of the English game. And thanks to Michael Owen's memorable intervention, the FA Cup had also been restored to *its* rightful place in the English footballing calendar as the crown jewel of the domestic season. Despite the demands of 21st-century football threatening to render it obsolete, the FA Cup retains a rare capacity to produce legends. To Owen belonged the ultimate tribute: 2001 will forever be remembered as the 'Owen Final', just as, for example, 1953 is revered as the 'Matthews Final'. For Owen and his team mates, however, the celebrations were on ice, as the players followed Gérard Houllier's orders to, as he described it, 'break with the traditional English culture' and abstain from alcohol for one more week, until the season's final two hurdles had been overcome: 'We've got to be professional, that's what our job is about and so the celebration will be so limited that it will be restricted to nothing,' Houllier said by way of explanation of a curfew that could certainly be described as a very limited way of celebrating!

Arsenal were a formidable but familiar foe, but what of Alavés, Liverpool's opponents in the UEFA Cup final? Gérard Houllier had done his homework on the relatively unknown Spaniards as thoroughly as one would have expected and knew, from the reports of club scout, Alex Miller, who had watched Alavés at the quarter-final stage, that they would be tough adversaries: 'He came back and told us we would probably be playing Alavés in the final,' Houllier explained. 'That's how highly he rated them. He predicted this final way back in March. I have heard it suggested that Alavés are just there to make up the numbers. That is not the case at all. We will not be making that mistake. If they are in the final it means they must be a good side, but unlike some people we were expecting them to reach the final. We set great store by what our scouts tell us.' Indeed, given that

Houllier had Liverpool's FA Cup semi-final opponents, Second Division Wycombe Wanderers, watched seven times, there was never any danger of him underestimating *Primera Liga* Alavés. Such an admission is classic Houllier, the master technocrat supreme. Barcelona, Manchester United, Wycombe – they are all just opponents, to be studied and respected. As Houllier has stated many times: 'In football, you cannot programme success. You can only prepare for it.' Whatever Houllier's scouts told him, it's a pretty near certainty that the dossier didn't envisage a chaotic end-to-end nine-goal thriller. The pundits, confidently predicting a dour 1–0 as the competition's two meanest defences squared up to one another, were equally bemused. Before the game, even the Alavés midfielder Jordi Cruyff got in on the act, by echoing his father's comments after the Nou Camp stalemate, alleging Liverpool were boring. The match, of course, turned out to be anything but, as Liverpool and Alavés traded punch for punch in nearly two hours of error-strewn, drama-filled football. The Reds, whose resilience was taking on mythic proportions, triumphed through a deep reserve of inner belief, greater discipline and through, crucially, possessing the flair at key moments to prise open their opponents' defence. The full story of the dramatic UEFA Cup triumph by the improbable score of 5–4 is told in Chapter 9 ('The Reds in Europe'). For Houllier and his players, the victory represented a significant achievement: 'That was an epic. We were playing for history tonight, for Liverpool's first European trophy in 17 years. The team played for immortality. Every player will be remembered for a long time.'

Liverpool's players and staff arrived back, jaded but elated by their triumph in the Westfalen Stadion, and went on, without time to pause for breath, to the final game of the season and a visit to the Valley for Liverpool's third cup final of the week. Fresh, if that is the right word, from their arduous encounter with Alavés, Gérard Houllier selected Fowler alongside Owen in attack and brought another impressive Dortmund substitute, Patrik Berger, into the starting eleven in place of the exhausted Hamann.

The first half was a very disjointed affair, as a tired Liverpool sought vainly to engage mind and body in the unified pursuit of their European ambition and Charlton squandered several good opportunities to take the lead. After half-time, however, Liverpool, dredging up one final reserve of energy, got quickly into their stride, and after Fowler had put the Reds in front with an inspired bicycle kick, there was never any doubt about the result. Owen and Fowler ran riot, carving open the Charlton defence at will, as Liverpool streamed forward, sealing their Champions League qualification in the most emphatic way possible with a 4–0 win. Houllier was overcome with emotion at the final whistle, embracing Thompson and his backroom staff on the touchline and congratulating each of his weary players separately on the pitch, before the team completed a well-deserved lap of honour to warm applause from both sets of supporters. The impossible had become reality for an overjoyed Gérard Houllier: 'This is a massive achievement. To finish third in the league and win three cups is wonderful. These players have made history this season. It was a massive performance. Before the game I thought the players were human – now I think they are super-human. They need a celebration now. They are tired and I am a bit tired myself. We have had to postpone the celebration until this game was out of the way and we will now look forward to a good get-together with the wives and girlfriends.'

Answering questions about Robbie Fowler's contribution to Liverpool's successful final week, two goals against Charlton, including the all-important first, and a stunning strike minutes after his arrival as a substitute against Alavés, Houllier responded a little defensively: 'He has never been close to leaving. I just said that if he wants to go then he goes. But it's not just about the manager. I'm pleased that he's said he knows there is competition but he wants to win things. If you want to be successful, you need four strikers.' With a clear reference to Fowler's omission from the two finals, Houllier went on: 'Robbie has shown a great team ethic in the past three games. You don't have to accept it [rotation] with a smile on your face, but you do have to understand it. I can prove that it pays off.'

As the squad and staff paraded around Liverpool city centre in an open-top bus before half a million onlookers with the spoils of three cup victories, like homecoming crusaders displaying their booty, who could deny that Gérard Houllier's strategy had indeed paid off – in spades. For Houllier, just a little over two and a half years into his five-year plan for the rebirth of Liverpool FC, it had been a truly memorable campaign, a season in which his tactics, from the much-maligned rotation policy to the equally derided counter-attacking game practised by his players, had brought unprecedented success to the club. Houllier outlined the extent to which the club had transcended the targets set at the team's pre-season Swiss training-camp: 'Both the players and technical staff had set out with the object of adding one trophy to the cabinet at the beginning of the season to provide proof of our progress. The fact that we were able to qualify for the Champions League one year ahead of schedule was therefore a major achievement. And we won three cups.' Yet, curious as it may now seem (particuarly given Sven-Goran Eriksson's whole-hearted embracing of exactly the same tactics in taking England to the quarter-finals of the 2002 World Cup), those triple cup successes came against a backdrop of criticism from fellow pros and rival managers, as well as the media. Some of it was well reasoned; much, however, smacked of jealousy or fear at the re-emergence of English football's sleeping giant.

Yet some of the criticism directed at the team that had just completed a prestigious and unparalleled triple cup triumph was not without justification. Halfway through the Houllier revolution, the manager's mid-term report could point, as its one caveat to set against the abundant positives, to the impression (borne particularly from the manner of those Cup final victories) of a team holding something back, a team that were successful, but, because of their cautious approach, only just so. It is undeniably true that luck played a part in Liverpool's remarkable cup success, particularly against Arsenal where, as even the most ardent Red will admit, the Gunners were for large parts of the game the superior team. Fortune, in the shape of a mysterious non-penalty decision, also helped Liverpool through their second-leg UEFA Cup tussle with Roma, and even where they were clearly the better team, they still struggled to beat Birmingham in the League Cup final, via the lottery of a penalty shoot-out, and Alavés in the UEFA Cup final, thanks to a 'golden goal' in extra time. Their performances in the domestic finals in particular begged the question, 'When are Liverpool going to get down to really playing?' Even in the more open, attack-minded game against Alavés Liverpool interspersed fluent sorties on their opponents' goal with a cautious approach, epitomised by Houllier's decision to bring Michael Owen off midway through the second period of normal time. This reluctance to go for the jugular of the opposition was as frustrating to watch as it was straining on the nerve-ends.

Ultimately, it comes down to tactics and personnel: Liverpool were not there yet and, in fairness to Houllier, nor were they supposed to be. In each area there remained room for improvement, no matter that, taken together, Liverpool's trophies built a powerful case for the quality of both. The midfield in particular lacked a little of the creativity and flair of their chief rivals Manchester United and Arsenal. With Hamann occupying a holding position with a remit that usually went no further than breaking up opposition attacks, Murphy prone to lapses in confidence and Smicer injury-plagued, the middle third remained the one area of the pitch where Liverpool fell a degree or two short. This is not to belittle the excellent contributions of Hamann, Murphy and Smicer to the Treble-winning success: each played their part to the full. Danny Murphy is, in fact, a fine example of a player who has made splendid strides forward under Houllier and, in so doing, amply repaid the manager's faith in him at a time when many observers openly questioned his future at Anfield.

But the line that runs between focusing on the players' capabilities and the style in which they are instructed to play is a fine one and, in Liverpool's case, further blurred by Houllier's frequent reliance on defence-minded tactics. The consequent deployment of the midfield four in a deep-lying position has often led to a breakdown in possession in the final third of the pitch, as Liverpool's forwards have become isolated from the midfield supply line. As a result, Liverpool have suffered a tendency to give the ball away cheaply. Battling for third place in the Premiership was one thing, but competing with the leading lights of the Champions League would represent another steep learning curve for Houllier's inexperienced side, and one where the ability to keep possession better and with a more positive emphasis on creating goalscoring openings would be essential if the Reds were to continue their steady, but perceptible, improvement under Houllier's careful tuition. The architect of the UEFA Cup final victory, Gary McAllister, recognised as much when he spoke, even in the euphoric aftermath of success, of the need for a much quicker supply of the ball to the forwards and, by implication, a much more positive approach to the game. Nonetheless, as the 2000–01 season drew to its close, Houllier was encouraged by the progress of his charges: 'We are already benefiting domestically from our European experience this season,' he explained. 'It is more difficult to win the UEFA Cup than the FA Cup, but it is all good experience. The important thing is to learn, and to keep taking the club forward.' Houllier was also at pains to point out the need for his team to continue their development, stressing that they were far from the finished article: 'You have to acknowledge the fact that Manchester United are a good side and they are getting bigger and bigger. We are not yet at their level, but I hope that in two or three years' time we can be. You have to be patient. Where we need to improve is patience in passing and movement.'

Champions League football would help Liverpool bridge that gap and take them nearer still to the Holy Grail of a sustained challenge to United for the Premiership title. Liverpool were now at a key phase in their redevelopment, ready to mount a creditable push for the title, buoyed by the experiences of the 2000–01 campaign. The resolve, focused mental attitude and sheer will to win demonstrated by Houllier's players was a throwback to a bygone era of relentless Liverpool success. 'The players have had so much to cope with, with all the different competitions,' Houllier said. 'Between the two legs of the Barcelona tie, for instance, we had three games. That's 5 games in 14 days. I must compliment the players at how well they have handled all the games. Their ability to compartmentalise, to keep each game, each competition, in a separate drawer, so to speak, has really stunned me.'

Equally impressive was, of course, Gérard Houllier's own contribution to Liverpool's monumental season. It therefore came as something of a shock when Houllier was passed over as Manager of the Year by the League Managers' Association in favour of Ipswich Town's George Burley. While Houllier was quick to congratulate Burley on his achievement (awarded on the back of leading Ipswich to a place in the UEFA Cup in their first season back in the Premiership), the fact remains that Burley and his club won nothing. Liverpool, by contrast, had made history by capturing three different trophies in the same season. The choice of Burley was, therefore, not only inappropriate, it also betrayed a reluctance on the part of the traditional footballing elements in England to recognise the impact on the British game brought about by the influx of high-calibre playing and coaching talent from abroad. Given John Barnwell's dismayed reaction to the appointment of Sven-Goran Eriksson as England boss a few months earlier, Houllier should not have been surprised by the outcome. Houllier was suitably stoical: 'To think, with all we have won, George Burley was voted Manager of the Year. There was no chance of that happening to me because I am foreign. In England, it is a culture shock when a foreign coach comes in. I understand that because you invented the game. But there is more pressure to prove yourself and I believe there is less tolerance for a foreign coach.'

Still, even if the League Managers' Association had failed to accord Monsieur Houllier his just reward, the people of Liverpool were happy to embrace the great Frenchman, whose love of Merseyside he had long proclaimed. While Liverpool's fans had played their part by gaining official recognition from UEFA for their sporting behaviour towards their Alavés counterparts in Dortmund, 'Le Boss' had returned to his footballing roots to restore to Liverpool FC the passion, spirit and, above all, the silverware that the club had grown accustomed to in the past and that, after a miserable decade of underachievement, many supporters feared had gone forever. Now, if he could just add a little more flair into the mix . . .

7

The Fowler Saga

Barely three months into the 2001–02 season and Liverpool were finally ready to offload Robbie Fowler. On Saturday, 24 November they made their intentions known to Leeds, the asking price a respectable £15 million. By Tuesday, 27 November, the Liverpool board – with Houllier's backing – had agreed to accept approximately £9.5 million up front with up to a further £3.5 million depending on appearances and honours. For a club renowned for its tough negotiation of transfer deals, on first inspection, this looked to supporters and neutrals alike an uncommonly poor piece of business. Of course, the McManaman episode was quoted endlessly by a defensive board. Liverpool could not let the same thing happen again. Fowler must not be allowed to run down the final 18 months on his contract and walk away on a Bosman, leaving Liverpool with nothing but memories and a stockpile of unused nose plasters. But the McManaman argument was a smokescreen. McManaman had wanted to leave, had never had any intention of putting pen to paper on a new contract. If Houllier could have persuaded McManaman to sign a new deal on the day his contract expired, Houllier would have jumped at the chance: money was no object; a guaranteed place in the first-team a given. There are no parallels with the Fowler situation. Liverpool wanted Robbie out and when the time was right he was allowed to leave. With almost indecent haste. No persuading, no negotiating.

Liverpool claimed Fowler's advisers were stalling on a new contract, but the club were paying no more than lip service to the idea (in his first interview after the move, Fowler categorically stated that he had never been offered a new deal – and the club never contradicted him). Top of the league, two points clear, a game in hand and five trophies in the bag, with Heskey having just played a key role in the 1–0 win over Sunderland that put the Reds clear at the top ('the players stood and applauded Emile into the dressing-room,' Phil Thompson pointedly remarked after the game) the time was finally right. The fans were appeased, behind Houllier all the way; Robbie could go.

What had brought things to such a head that as skilful and popular a footballer as Fowler, a man idolised in his native Merseyside, was allowed to leave Liverpool with no more than a resigned shrug, a pat on the back and a 'good luck at your new club' message from the manager? The answer is not all that straightforward but, in essence, the sale of Liverpool's favourite son was sanctioned by Gérard Houllier because he had grown tired of waiting for Robbie Fowler to recapture the mercurial form of his early years at Anfield. The evidence suggests that, by Christmas 2000, the board had given up hope of ever seeing the renaissance of Fowler's striking talents and were prepared to let him go. Certainly, Houllier had tried hard in his first two seasons at Liverpool to integrate Fowler into his new, counter-attacking team pattern but Fowler's inconsistent form, susceptibility to injury and inability to regain full fitness as quickly as Houllier would have liked, ultimately frustrated him. Nonetheless, Houllier stood by his errant striker, through Fowler's many on- and off-field transgressions, claiming, with some justification, that 'no manager could have been more supportive of Robbie over the years'. Eventually, his patience wore thin, Owen's consistent brilliance eclipsed Fowler's fading star and, in Heskey and Litmanen, Houllier gave himself other striking options.

In his final 12 months at Anfield, Fowler became increasingly marginalised, his opportunities to stake a claim for a place in Liverpool's starting line-up ever more restricted. If Robbie has cause for feeling any resentment or bitterness at his treatment by Houllier then it is in respect of those final few months when, no matter what he did on the pitch, he invariably found himself 'rotated' out of the starting line-up shortly thereafter. Patently third choice behind Houllier's preferred Owen–Heskey coalition, deemed an unsuitable strike partner for the Boy Wonder, lacking the pace necessary to team up with Litmanen, the one man whose vision would have created the openings he craved, Robbie Fowler was denied any real opportunity to prove his worth to Houllier in a consistent run of matches during his final year at Liverpool. His reward for being the first man to score a Premiership hat trick in 2001–02 was a place on the bench for the next three games. Yet, even during this period, Fowler oscillated between moments of sublime excellence (such as the League Cup-winning goal against Birmingham, his strike against Alavés in the UEFA Cup, or the inspired overhead kick which set Liverpool on their way to victory at Charlton on the final day of the 2000–01 season) and strangely out-of-sorts displays characterised by misplaced passes, sluggish movement and an air of resignation that suggested he fully expected the substitute's board to be raised aloft with his number on it at any moment. The football world looked on in a state of bemusement as Liverpool and Fowler played out the most public and attenuated of divorces, the breakdown in relations epitomised by the club's decision to give a public airing to what should have remained a behind-closed-doors incident (the training ground bust-up with Phil Thompson that precipitated Fowler's eventual transfer).

In fact, Houllier, who took over the reins at Anfield just a few months after Michael Owen had first lit up the world stage, only ever saw glimpses of the best of Robbie Fowler in the three years he had him under his charge. Owen's startling ascendancy was the beginning of the end for the 'Toxteth Terror'. Robbie always had a strange kind of vulnerability that the Liverpool fans warmed to and Owen's arrival on the scene wormed away at his self-belief, undermining his status as golden boy. His insecurity was odd, because, for one so talented, Fowler appeared liable to self-doubt. Unlike the preternaturally mature Owen, bashful Robbie was nervous and self-effacing in front of the cameras, one moment rationalising his failure to be awarded a hat trick against West Ham (having had a perfectly good third goal chalked out) as a blessing for his father ('he doesn't have room for another match ball in the house anyway'), the next claiming that criticism was bound to affect him, that all he wanted was a chance to prove himself. By the beginning of the 2001–02 season, alas, that chance had gone.

By then, the club had decided to sell Fowler before things reached the point of no return and the player's transfer value had been eroded by the running down of his contract. It is worth emphasising again, however, that this was a completely different situation from that which provoked the loss of McManaman for nothing: here, the club held the whip hand and were the driving force. By contrast, if he had felt there was any realistic prospect of featuring regularly in Houllier's plans, Fowler would have been happy to sign a new contract. In wrongly emphasising the parallels with the McManaman episode, Liverpool misled their supporters. The board, fearful of Fowler's undiminished status as cult hero at Anfield, were guilty of pulling the wool over the fans' eyes with regard to their commitment to offering Fowler a new deal, when clearly one was not forthcoming. But aside from a little public relations massaging (and why exacerbate a potentially difficult situation by stirring up the passions of the supporters at a time when the club needed to pull together during Houllier's convalescence?), in deciding to sell Fowler, Liverpool acted with good sense, in the best interests of the team and, in accepting that Robbie needed regular first-team football, to the player's advantage as well. Houllier, speaking publicly (at Liverpool's December AGM) for the first time since his hospitalisation, summarised the dilemma from Fowler's viewpoint: 'It was clear that Robbie was unhappy at not being an automatic first choice. He obviously wants to play in next year's World Cup and believes that playing more regularly will allow him to do that. I will not keep a player at this club who is unhappy.'

The transfer of Robbie Fowler was absolutely the right move for both club and player. However, the sale of a star player to bitter championship rivals Leeds was always going to be a politically difficult move for Houllier. That the transfer was made while the Frenchman was at home recuperating from open-heart surgery, out of the media glare but with the sympathies of everyone in football, and with Liverpool top of the Premiership for the first time in Houllier's stewardship, was no coincidence. The reality is that for the first time in three years Houllier felt able to cut the umbilical cord that tied the Kop to its favourite son. That Houllier, in an age of Diomedes, Arphexads and Biscans, felt comfortable enough to ratify the sale of the local boy made good says much for the club's determination to relinquish its one-time prize asset.

All the same, the *Liverpool Echo* of Wednesday, 28 November 2001, the fateful day of the move, was inundated with irate letters from grieving supporters, many enraged that not only had their hero been sold, but his destination was Leeds United. Liverpool's decision to accept Leeds' £13 million bid was a calculated risk, even though, in agreeing the deal, Liverpool were conceivably providing Leeds with the cutting edge that would return the title to Elland Road and extend Liverpool's own barren championship years. But, given Liverpool had resolved to sell Fowler, they could hardly be expected to offload him to Blackburn (as was mooted). Why would a player of Fowler's calibre agree to such a move? As Houllier put it, 'Robbie decided he wanted to move to Leeds and you have to respect his decision. The fact he went to Elland Road is not important. I am more concerned about my squad than that of others.' Short of Leeds winning the title themselves – *and* on the back of Robbie's goals – Houllier could live with the consequences of his actions. To claim, as at least one national newspaper did, 'now Liverpool must win the title or Houllier is finished', was bordering on the sensational. Still, Leeds *were* realistic contenders for the title and, coming just weeks after a massive life-saving operation, the decision to sell the man the supporters referred to as 'God' was as brave a move as Houllier had made in his tenure at the club, dwarfing his decision to release Ince, James and other stalwarts of the Evans era.

Despite the furious reaction the transfer provoked among many Liverpool fans, there was also a sizeable minority who were able to view the deal with something approaching equanimity. True, Robbie Fowler remained the most popular player at the club (his warming up on the touchline during his increasingly frequent substitute appearances under Houllier invariably brought louder cheers from the Kop than the on-field exploits of his team mates), but in the cold light of day, it was hard to escape the feeling that Fowler's best moments in the red shirt were behind him. It was strange, but it felt like Fowler had been at Liverpool forever. Because persistent injuries had robbed him of so much time on the pitch since a serious collision with the Everton goalkeeper Thomas Myhre in February 1998, it made Fowler's early, extraordinary goalscoring exploits legendary, shrouded in nostalgia. It was hard to believe that he was still only 26.

Yet, no matter how one rationalised it, no matter how much the head said it was the right move for Liverpool, the heart said otherwise. The fans still regarded the Toxteth-born striker as one of their own, a supporter fulfilling the dream. And through all his follies and traumas, the love affair between player and supporters had never wavered. Stephen Birley, writing in the *Guardian* after Fowler's departure, captured the essence of the man's appeal: 'There are players, and Fowler is certainly one of them, who, like certain actors or musicians, always and magically make the onlooker feel part of what they are doing.' The self-deprecating Fowler, by turns humorous and melancholic, was revered and cherished in a way that, up until then at least, the brilliant Michael Owen could not have claimed to be.

The potential ramifications of the transfer meant Liverpool would have considered every other option before finally deciding to sell Fowler, especially to Leeds. While the sale of a star player still at, or just past, his peak had its precedent in the transfers of Keegan, Aldridge and Ian Rush, all had been sold abroad (to Hamburg, Real Sociedad and Juventus respectively), never to a rival for the title. Arguably, the Fowler move also contained an element of risk for David O'Leary. But if the enigmatic Fowler could rediscover his best form at Elland Road, it had all the makings of Leeds' own version of the deal done many years ago in Yorkshire that allowed Eric Cantona to cross the Pennines to rewrite Manchester United's history. Ironically, Cantona's move to English football was brokered by Houllier, who, in conjunction with Michel Platini, talked Cantona out of quitting the game altogether after he had been suspended for violent conduct by the French football authorities. Howard Wilkinson, then in charge at Leeds, rang Houllier to ask for his opinion on the capricious Frenchman and, on the back of Houllier's glowing reference, signed him immediately. Later, after Cantona and Wilkinson had fallen out, Houllier was instrumental in Cantona making his fateful journey to Old Trafford, telephoning Alex Ferguson to advise him of Cantona's availability. Houllier, then, will surely have remembered that Wilkinson was finished as Leeds' manager in the eyes of the supporters the day Eric Cantona lifted the Premiership trophy at the end of his first season with Manchester United.

The same year that Cantona moved to Old Trafford to inspire United to a new era of dominance in English football, a young Robbie Fowler made his Liverpool debut as an impudent 18 year old in a League Cup tie at Fulham. He scored, of course, in a 3–1 first-leg victory and announced his emergence with all five goals in Liverpool's 5–0 second-leg win at Anfield. Fowler's celebrations were not excessive: 'After the game, I went round the chippy with my mates and got a big kiss from my mum when I got home!' Liverpool's manager, Graeme Souness (addressing a curious media), was succinct: 'He's not coming out. He said he wouldn't know what to say.'

Over the course of the next four years, Robbie Fowler's performances for Liverpool were (even to the eyes of an unbiased spectator) simply magnificent. He helped make Liverpool, along with his close friend Steve McManaman and later, Stan Collymore, the most exciting team in the country. Goals rained in from all angles, with all manner of finishes, from the nonchalant to the delicate to the thunderous; goals scored clinically with either foot (although he favoured his left), headers, volleys, lobs, a natural predator's close-range tap-ins, even Beckhamesque free kicks before Golden Balls was a twinkle in Posh Spice's eye. He scored against the best too – hat tricks against Arsenal's miserly defence in successive seasons, four goals in two games against Manchester United's double-winning side of 1995–96. In all, Robbie Fowler played in 188 games and scored 116 goals in those first 4 heady seasons.

Among the many highlights, several feats stand out: Robbie's four goals in a 5–1 victory over Middlesbrough, the first, inside the opening few seconds of the game, greeted by Fowler and McManaman grinning, pointing at their wrists to check imaginary watches. The audacious strike in a Cup Winners' Cup tie against Brann, when Fowler flicked the ball over a startled defender with the back of his heel before turning and volleying in one movement into the bottom corner of the net from the cutest of angles. A brace at Old Trafford to overshadow Cantona in his comeback match; the first goal a razor-sharp drive from the far corner of the penalty area, the second a deftly executed chip over Schmeichel. Two stunning strikes against Aston Villa in the FA Cup semi-final. The fastest hat trick in Premiership history (four and a half minutes!) against Arsenal at Anfield. And each goal greeted with the same boyish, undiluted glee of a born goalscorer, a man who lived off the gratification of seeing the ball hit the back of the net.

Fowler's obvious delight at scoring was just one of the many facets of his on-field personality that so endeared him to his Liverpool public. Other eccentric, but typically heartfelt, moments helped win over the neutrals.

Twice in the space of a week during the tense run-in to the 1996–97 campaign, Fowler was involved in a bizarre episode. First, in a rare display of political allegiance (unless bedding the daughter of a Labour MP qualifies as a political statement), he scored a goal in a Cup Winners' Cup match at Anfield and revealed a T-shirt which read, in the style of the Calvin Klein logo of the time, 'Support the 500 Sacked Dockers'. Fowler had been given the T-shirt by McManaman (who was also wearing one). Macca explained, 'A friend of my dad's was one of the 500 workers sacked. I thought I would wear it under my shirt, merely as a small statement of support for people, some of whom are friends, not as a grand gesture.' The pair were amazed by the media's hysterical reaction to the incident, and Fowler's subsequent fining by UEFA. A few days later, in a titanic clash at Highbury, Robbie was seemingly brought down in the box by Arsenal's David Seaman. The referee promptly awarded the penalty, only for Robbie to repeatedly plead with him, in front of a stunned North Bank, that no foul had been committed. Fowler, clearly affected by the incident, purposefully or otherwise, missed the penalty. This time he received a FIFA Fair Play award for his act of great sportsmanship.

Unfortunately, the 1996–97 season was to be Robbie Fowler's final injury-free, free-scoring campaign in a Liverpool shirt. The origins of his problems can be traced back to the summer of 1997: an injury in a pre-season game in Norway, meaning he was out of commission for the first two months of the new season; the loss of his strike partner Stan Collymore; the emergence of Michael Owen in Fowler's early season absence; and the increasing transfer speculation surrounding his best friend and team mate Steve McManaman. There was also the disappointment of finishing fourth in a two-horse race the previous season, combined with the distressing defeat in the Cup Winners' Cup semi-final to Paris St Germain, as the 1996–97 season fell apart at its climax. With the previous year's dismal FA Cup final capitulation to Manchester United fresh in the memory, it seemed as though Liverpool – and Robbie – had lost their chance of winning major trophies under Roy Evans. The team seemed to choke too often on the big occasion.

1997–98 was a difficult time for Robbie. After starting the season late, he quickly hit form, only for the goals to dry up in the New Year. Then came the injury against Everton which was to end his season prematurely. He was out of action until September, and during this time lost his mantle as the player all schoolboys wanted to be on the playground. Suddenly, Michael Owen was the star, and his dashing good looks appealed to the girls as well. In the summer's World Cup, while Fowler stayed at home nursing his injury ('I think that missing out on the World Cup in 1998 was one of the worst moments of my career. It was a devastating moment when I realised I wouldn't be going'), Owen shot to national and worldwide fame with his performances for England. For those beyond Merseyside, it was Owen's name with which Liverpool FC became associated. It was Owen who had the big boot deals, who starred in TV commercials. It must have been hard for Fowler to see his perceived status as leading man wrestled from him. Prior to that 1997–98 season he had been virtually indispensable, the first name on Roy Evans' team sheet for four years. Now he faced an uncertain future, as he sought to regain his former sharpness under a new managerial set-up.

Within a month of Fowler's return to the first-team, while he was still some way short of full fitness, Roy Evans had resigned and Liverpool were under the sole custody of Gérard Houllier. Liverpool swiftly moved towards a different, more defensive style of football under their new, disciplinarian French coach, with the emphasis placed on quick counter-attacking. Fowler no longer had an endless supply of crosses and knock-downs from Collymore, McAteer and McManaman to feed off. Indeed, the departure of McManaman to Real Madrid at the end of Houllier's first season in charge was a particularly big blow for Robbie, off as well as on the pitch. They were, of course, best friends who spent hours following, with increasing fervour, their favourite pastime outside football: horseracing. The 'Anfield Hombres' became co-owners, with the assistance of champion jockey Tony McCoy, of a filly they named dryly 'Some Horse', just so they could hear commentators say 'and Some Horse has won by a photo finish' and watch bewildered punters wonder which horse it was exactly. Predictably, they then bought another horse, and called it 'Another Horse'. Alas, 'Growler' would have to make do without such japes in the future!

It was not just the loss of McManaman that hit Robbie hard. Other drinking buddies, like Matteo, Babb, James and McAteer, were shipped out by Houllier and replaced with sociable but sober Europeans. Suddenly Fowler, who was not averse to the occasional glass of shandy, was alone at Anfield and unable to bond so easily with the likes of Smicer, Henchoz and Hyypiä, who preferred a meal with their wives to a pub crawl – when the manager allowed them to drink at all, that is. Mini-bars were emptied in advance of hotel visits, mobile phones were banned from the training ground; there was suddenly a new work ethic at Melwood. Gone were the days when a player could park in the manager's space, pelt him with mud or turn up late.

As Fowler struggled to cope with the new regime at Anfield, he made life increasingly awkward for himself by becoming embroiled in a succession of controversial incidents, beginning with a deranged five-week spell in the spring of 1999, when he managed to get himself banned for the final six games of the season after first flaunting his backside at Graeme Le Saux and then pretending to snort cocaine in a novel goal celebration against Everton. Whilst serving his suspension, he was assaulted while drinking in a Liverpool hotel bar and suffered facial injuries as a consequence. Houllier's anger was inflamed by the fact that Fowler had been out drinking when the incident occurred: 'The problem is that players think they can drink. Drinking alcohol is as silly as putting diesel in a racing car.' Even when not playing, Fowler, much to Houllier's undisguised irritation, continued to make headlines for the wrong reasons.

Back on the pitch, Fowler was unable to forge any kind of partnership with Owen as one or the other was always injured. Ordered in by Houllier for extra training during the summer in a bid to regain full fitness, Fowler started the 1999–2000 campaign brightly, with a match-winning display against Arsenal. However, another setback to his damaged knee meant more surgery and he barely figured for the remainder of the season. Frustrated by his lack of action, he finally returned in time for the curious dénouement when Liverpool failed to score in any of their last five games and consequently missed out on a Champions League place. Fowler refused to join the lap of honour at the conclusion of the final home game after being substituted. As punishment, his latest journey through the pique district led to him being dropped, even from the bench, for the last match against Bradford, despite Champions League qualification hinging on the game.

As the 2000–01 season dawned, the consensus of opinion within the club's hierarchy was that Robbie's Liverpool career had reached breaking point. He had to stay out of trouble off the field, while rediscovering his talent for scoring goals on it. And he had to stay clear of injuries. Unfortunately, he managed none of these. The long, painfully slow, diminishing of his talent continued – at least Fowler's increasingly irregular appearances on the pitch suggested it did. Robbie struggled to regain his best form. By December, the board had decided to cut their losses and were prepared to accept Chelsea's £12 million bid for the player. Houllier, forever the doctrinaire strategist, used the situation to his advantage, casually informing Fowler, 'We have had a bid from Chelsea – do you want to talk to them?' The ploy worked; Fowler's belief that he was too important to be discarded was shattered. Houllier followed this up a few weeks later by telling Robbie that he was also free to explore an offer from Aston Villa. Houllier had made his point – Fowler was dispensable. Not that Houllier would have sanctioned a move at that juncture. His side were fighting for trophies on three fronts and were confronted by a fixture back-log. He needed Robbie to stay and besides, he insisted Fowler would only be allowed to move if he put in a transfer request of his own. If Liverpool instigated the sale, Fowler would be entitled to a pay-off in the region of £2 million. If Fowler chose to go voluntarily, he would waive his right to this payment. An uneasy stand-off developed, with Chelsea, Aston Villa and Leeds all monitoring the situation closely. Publicly, Fowler remained keen to stay at Anfield, saying: 'I want it known that I am happy at Liverpool at the minute. I don't think I even need to say that. Obviously from the playing point of view I could be happier, but that just means I've got to knuckle down more.' He set about shedding his excess pounds and convincing his manager that he could rise to the level of fitness and dedication Houllier demanded. Fowler's resolve to reclaim his place in Liverpool's starting eleven was such that he pushed himself through double sessions in training, and even volunteered for extra solo shifts.

A week later Houllier must have been questioning the wisdom of his decision to turn down Chelsea's offer. Fowler was once more the victim of an unprovoked attack, this time at two in morning; the location, outside one of Liverpool's less salubrious bars, beggared belief. He was given his final warning and dropped from the next three games by a furious Houllier who, although remaining scrupulously careful not to overdo the public admonishment, could not mask his annoyance, even when ostensibly offering Fowler support in the press: 'I feel great sympathy for Robbie and everyone at the club is fully supportive of him at this time. Okay, we have to acknowledge he was probably in the wrong place at that time, but nevertheless it was a completely unprovoked attack.' This time, Robbie knew he had gone too far.

The day after the assault, which again left Fowler sporting nasty facial injuries, Liverpool announced that they had captured the Barcelona star Jari Litmanen on a free transfer. Speculation intensified over Fowler's future following the arrival of Litmanen, but Houllier insisted, unconvincingly, that the situation remained as before: 'My position on Robbie Fowler has not changed. Everybody knows what I think about that. I said I wanted four strikers and we have that with Jari's arrival.'

Rotation had now become the buzzword at Anfield and with Liverpool increasingly looking to utilise the pace of Heskey and Owen on the break, rotation, more often than not, seemed to mean dropping Robbie Fowler. Heskey was never 'rotated' (with the exception of a game against Ipswich); Owen was rested rather than rotated to give his fragile hamstrings the chance to recover from playing. Now, with Litmanen, a fourth high-calibre striker had been added to the equation. For Fowler, rotation was a source of immense, and understandable, frustration, particularly as he was showing signs of getting back to somewhere near his regal best, as his wonder strike in the League Cup final against Birmingham demonstrated.

Despite Fowler's continued traumas and his own misgivings, Houllier seemed desperately to want Fowler to do well, remaining willing to have him captain the team (on those occasions when he was actually playing) during Redknapp's permanent absence. When he scored the winning goal against Chelsea in a League Cup tie, the pair were dancing 'high fives' on the touchline. After finally getting on the scoresheet in the 5–0 demolition of Crystal Palace in the semi-final of the same competition, Houllier spoke of his joy that Fowler had found the net after such a virtuoso performance. His team mates also appeared keen for him to succeed. The Crystal Palace match featured an amazing miss by Litmanen, when the Finn spurned the opportunity of a first goal for his new club in front of the Kop in favour of heading back across an open goal for the less well-placed Robbie to score (he didn't!).

Still, no matter how positive or public his manager's eulogising, Fowler remained unable to accept being left out for tactical reasons. And with success for the team came more opportunities for resentment, none more so than being omitted from the starting line-up for Liverpool's two biggest matches in years: the FA and UEFA Cup finals. Fowler was, naturally, upset that Heskey – who had been at the club barely a year and, on current form, did not merit a place in the side – was starting ahead of him. Fortunately for Robbie, and the team, he was able to get on in both matches, scoring after a twisting run and deadly accurate finish with his weaker right foot against Alavés in the UEFA Cup final to put his team 4–3 up on the way to extra-time victory. Concluding the season with two goals at Charlton, Liverpool and Fowler finished on a high, with their place in the Champions League assured. Robbie was keen to extend his contract and elated at his welcome back into the international fold under Sven-Goran Eriksson.

Fowler's England career, after being handed his first cap by Terry Venables as a 21 year old in 1996 against Bulgaria, had never really blossomed. He was restricted, understandably, to a couple of brief cameos in Euro '96 by the partnership of Shearer and Sheringham. When Sheringham's form dipped prior to the World Cup finals of 1998, Fowler's chance of replacing him already lay in ruins through injury, opening the door instead for his club colleague Michael Owen. It was an opportunity Owen took with relish and, over the next couple of years, his consistently dazzling performances for his country helped keep Fowler in the shade. A succession of England managers – Venables, Hoddle and Keegan – expressed their admiration for Fowler's abilities yet used him sparingly.

Owen's success for Liverpool and England provoked questions about his on- and off-field relationship with Robbie Fowler. Critics maintained that Fowler and Owen were just too similar in style to be compatible strike partners. Yet they played together on too few occasions – just 10 times out of 63 games in the Treble-winning season – to give credence to that theory. In those matches when they did play together, the results were not always good, but as the last-day 4–0 win at Charlton amply demonstrated, could be breathtaking. Fowler was convinced that he and Owen could work interchangeably in a split-striker partnership, believing the fact that Owen is predominantly right-footed and he left-footed to be another advantage, much like having a left- and a right-hander at the crease together. 'Michael and I have played that way before and he is very, very good at it,' Fowler said. 'Both of us can play outside the box and switch positions.'

A lot was also made of the fact that Fowler and Owen did not appear to hit it off. But whatever the truth in such rumours (and in all probability Fowler saw Owen as a rival for a place in the Liverpool and England attack, but no more than that), Fowler went into what would turn out to be his final season at Anfield more optimistic about the future than at any time in the past three years. The club were now finally equipped to mount a credible challenge for the title and Robbie wanted to be part of it. Yet, even before the season's traditional curtain raiser, the Charity Shield, could get underway, Fowler was again in serious trouble and a question mark hung over his Anfield future once more. The source of the latest chapter in the never-ending saga that was Robbie Fowler's career at Liverpool FC was, of all the childish and ridiculous things, a training-ground spat with assistant manager, Phil Thompson.

The incident started after Fowler hit a ball close to Thompson's head during penalty practice at the end of a training session. Fowler explained: 'I was taking penalties into one of the goals where Phil Thompson was fixing down the net. One flew into the corner and the ball just missed Phil.' Fowler will go no further than to admit that a heated exchange took place between the two. An eyewitness, however, recounts that Thompson 'came out shouting and screaming that Robbie had deliberately tried to hit him. Robbie replied that if he had been trying to hit Phil he would have taken his head off and the row degenerated from there. Phil shouted something about Robbie having been with the club too long and that the time had maybe come for him to move on. That is what really upset Robbie.' Fowler was equally distraught that Houllier had broken his promise to play him in the Charity Shield and that he had missed out on a winner's medal as a result. Thompson reported the row to Houllier who decided to make it into a very public cause célèbre. Fowler was banished from the side until, like a naughty schoolboy on suspension, he had apologised to Mr Thompson in Headmaster Houllier's office.

The Melwood incident overshadowed the opening-day fixture against West Ham. Fowler was watching from the Main Stand and was the first name chanted by the Kop for the new season. He left his seat with five minutes to go to a standing ovation. Speaking after the game, Houllier was unyielding: 'Robbie is acting as if he doesn't want Liverpool, as if he doesn't want the good of Liverpool. If he wants the good of Liverpool he has to shake hands and it's finished. If he does that, then obviously there is no problem. But regarding my position, there is no change. If it is not resolved we will have to see, but don't expect me to soften.'

Fowler felt bullied, describing the incident as 'trivial and stupid' and expressing his dismay that it had been heavily publicised by the club. Eventually, sensing that Houllier was not bluffing, he decided to climb down and made his apologies. Houllier responded by saying 'Robbie has done well to make his peace.' The feeling remained, however, that this otherwise innocuous incident (of a kind which happens on training grounds every day up and down the country) had been deliberately manipulated by Liverpool to push Fowler to the brink. This suspicion was quickly reinforced. No sooner had Fowler returned to the side than he was again publicly chided by his manager for his lack of form and fitness: 'Robbie is not fit enough and now he has to pick himself up and produce better football all round. We are all aware that he needs to improve his football, and he knows better than anyone. He's capable of it but it is down to him.'

It was true that Fowler did not suit the rotation system. He seemed unable to knuckle down and regain full fitness when he was not playing games and when he did emerge from the bench for the final ten minutes of matches, he often looked ponderous and disinterested. His tendency to indulge in obvious displays of petulance (visible head-shaking when substituted, disappointment etched into his face; sighing and wincing when passes didn't come off or moves broke down) alienated even some of his staunchest apologists, who felt, with some justification, that it shouldn't prove beyond someone earning a reported £40,000 a week to put up with whatever Houllier threw at him.

Fowler, naturally, wanted to play every minute of every game. As, of course, did Owen, whose attitude, on the few occasions he was omitted, remained exemplary. After suffering heavy concussion in a game at Derby, Owen was sidelined for a few weeks and on his return, went through a rare rough patch, missing chances he would normally have taken with ease. His response was to push himself even harder. Owen, relentlessly devoted to the pursuit of excellence, felt he had to be performing at the peak of his physical fitness, had to eradicate every possible weakness from his game. Whereas, in the current climate at Anfield, especially in the aftermath of the training ground affair, Fowler's response to being dropped was to sulk. His morale was damaged by his demotion to 'squad member' and he found it hard to work at his game when he felt he was not first choice to partner Owen. Fowler's nominal status as captain of the side served to further disillusion him. 'He [Houllier] made me captain, which was a great honour, but I used to go in and see him and ask him, "how many captains at other Premier League clubs do you see sitting on the bench?" There's not an answer to that, to be honest. When you are sitting on a bench, you're not a captain, are you? The fact is that I was third choice. It was obvious that I wasn't in the first-choice team Gérard wanted to play.'

Fowler was privately distraught at Houllier's latest public coal-raking. He managed a dignified response, stating he was working as hard as he could to rediscover his form, but from this moment on he and his advisers knew that there was no point in attempting to negotiate a new contract at Liverpool – not that one appeared to be forthcoming. Although neither Houllier nor Thompson would openly admit as much, Fowler was being forced out of Anfield. (After the dust had settled on his move to Leeds, Fowler was candid: 'I still get on very well with Gérard and I don't want to say he forced me out, but I think people can read between the lines.') With the 2002 World Cup looming and his last opportunity to play on the game's biggest stage slipping away, the time had come for Robbie to make the decision he had hoped he would never have to make – to leave his boyhood club and adoring fans.

Houllier's emergency heart operation and some fine performances (including a hat trick against Leicester) muddied the waters but it was obvious that, under Phil Thompson's temporary stewardship, things weren't about to get a whole lot better. Fowler remained marginalised, Owen kept scoring goals, Heskey endured a lengthy goal drought but remained a constant in the team. The only thing stopping Fowler leaving was the game of Russian Roulette being played by player and club – who would move first? Would Fowler forego his right to a £2 million signing-off fee or would Liverpool accept paying it in order to bring matters to a head?

Finally, Liverpool informed Leeds (Houllier and O'Leary had a close relationship and spoke regularly) that they were prepared to part with their talisman. A fee was hastily agreed and, with a speed that surprised even Liverpool officials, Fowler was arriving at Elland Road for a medical and the media was awash with 'Fowler to Leeds!' stories within days. After years of upheaval, of rumours and counter-rumours, and endless press speculation concerning Fowler's future, when the moment finally arrived, the transfer, while highly emotive, was an anti-climax. Houllier took advantage of his enforced absence from the spotlight to slip Fowler out quietly by the back door. The move's real drama lay in its potential implications for Houllier and Liverpool, and for the championship race that lay ahead.

On Friday, 30 November 2001, three years to the month that Gérard Houllier had taken sole charge of Liverpool, Robbie Fowler was unveiled at a packed press conference as a Leeds United player. Looking slightly bemused by the rapid turn of events, Fowler spoke softly and with no hint of malice in his voice: 'It was fairly obvious how things have panned out. Things haven't gone well for me. I have been at Liverpool a long time. They were always magnificent to me but I needed a new challenge.' Both publicly and privately, the divorce was not as acrimonious as it might once have been. Houllier stated later, 'I like him as a person and we got on well which is why I rang him before his Leeds debut to wish him all the best in this new stage in his career and tell him that he would always be welcome at Melwood.' By now it was in the interests of both parties to move on as quickly as possible.

Robbie Fowler's Liverpool affair was over. 'God has left the building,' as one banner unveiled at the next home game proclaimed, but although events in the short-term suggested that Gérard Houllier had been very wrong indeed, ultimately the move was to prove the right one for both Liverpool and Robbie. Not that Liverpool's supporters believed so initially: within weeks, Robbie, linking up effectively with Mark Viduka, and looking slimmer and sharper than he had for months, was scoring freely at

Leeds, as Liverpool's title challenge foundered on a poor run of just one win – and seven goals – garnered in nine Premiership games, since his departure. During that time, Liverpool relinquished an eleven-point lead over Manchester United and slipped from first to fifth. But there were many factors behind that disappointing sequence of results, not least Gérard Houllier's own (thankfully, temporary) absence from Merseyside.

And while the goals continued to come in a steady stream for Fowler, his new club fared less well, hitting a slump in form in the New Year that saw their title aspirations all but extinguished by the beginning of March. Fowler-less Liverpool, meanwhile, having pulled themselves out of their mid-season rut, went from strength to strength to secure a well-deserved runners-up berth. Liverpool may not have won the Premiership, but they had finished the season strongly. The goals dried up for Fowler as Leeds ended the campaign 14 points behind the Reds and outside the Champions League places. With each passing day, Houllier's decision to sell Fowler had appeared more and more judicious, while for his part, a regular starting place at Elland Road had gone a long way to ensuring Robbie Fowler a place in England's World Cup squad.

8

Modern Liverpool

Gérard Houllier's reign as Liverpool manager has been marked by a transformation in the club's commercial status, from a family-run business to a multi-media enterprise at the cutting-edge of new technology. Liverpool have embraced the digital age arguably more fervently than any other club and with an entrepreneur's willingness to try new ventures. It was the Reds' groundbreaking deal with Granada which paved the way for other football clubs to give up an ownership stake in return for capital investment and expertise in marketing and the exploitation of assets and rights. And it was Liverpool who became the first club in world football to screen a match live on the internet (the game against Manchester United at Old Trafford in February 2002) by webcasting it to their fanbase across the globe.

Set against this pioneering spirit, geared to unearthing new revenue streams from the utilisation of increasingly valuable global rights, modern Liverpool remains conscious of the need to avoid fleecing its fans. As Gérard Houllier's team consumes trophies with an ever more voracious appetite, so the money-spinning potential of those rights grows. So far, Liverpool have more or less succeeded in balancing the fans' interests against the drive to maximise the commercial worth of the club. However, the aggressive marketing of the Liverpool brand has, at times, left a slightly bad taste in the mouths of Reds supporters, who, better than most, appreciate the traditional values of the game.

Inevitably, under Rick Parry's stewardship as Chief Executive (Parry, remember, was at least partly responsible for the 1990s football 'boom', having negotiated the Sky television contract on behalf of the Premiership),

Liverpool have become more proactive and dynamic in the arena of exploiting the club's image through a plethora of broadcasting, merchandise and sponsorship deals.

The first of these was cemented in July 1999, as Liverpool announced 'a ground-breaking strategic partnership' with Granada. To date, it remains the biggest deal the club has ever been party to. At a price of £22.1 million, Granada purchased a 9.9 per cent share in Liverpool FC. As part of the agreement, the broadcasting conglomerate attained the right to manage a wide range of commercial issues for the club, focusing on publishing, electronic media rights and merchandising. The agreement was cleverly structured from several points of view. Liverpool was able to retain its status as a private, family-run company (chairman David Moores remained in control of the club, with his stake reduced from 58 per cent to 51 per cent), while raising significant funds to underwrite Houllier's squad revamp and further develop the Academy. In Granada, Liverpool had a powerful media ally, able to take on a range of business functions at the club and exploit the Liverpool FC brand, thus freeing its management to concentrate on achieving success on the field.

From Granada's point of view, the deal made sense on various levels: it gave Granada influence within the club, as and when the television rights for Premiership matches came up for renewal, and placed them in pole position for delivering digital pay-per-view coverage of matches, for the time when clubs will be allowed to sell their own rights to individual games (ultimately, the aim is to create a dedicated Liverpool FC television channel). For Liverpool's fans, the pleasure of seeing their club tie up a lucrative source of team-building revenue was enhanced by the timing of the announcement, coming as it did just a few weeks after BSkyB's very public failure to take over Manchester United.

One year on from the original agreement, Liverpool and Granada's strategic alliance entered phase two with Granada Media's purchase of a 50 per cent share in Liverpool's official website, liverpoolfc.tv, enabling the company to take half of all revenues generated from subscription, merchandising and advertising sources. With football clubs acquiring the right to show highlights and delayed coverage of their own games from the commencement of the 2001–02 season, the long-term focus of this new arrangement was the online webcasting of live matches. Granada Media's input was quickly felt, as the club wasted no time in building on the mushrooming in popularity of football coverage on the internet, launching the 'e-season ticket' which enables fans to view player interviews, goal highlights and other special features for an annual subscription. Boosted by the success of the team under Houllier and aided by the presence at the club of high-profile stars like Owen, Heskey and Gerrard, the website has quickly attained a healthy worldwide audience (although the majority still prefer to use the site's more restricted but free facilities).

Liverpool have also sought to expand revenue from more established means through licensing traditional broadcasting rights and sales of replica kits. The main television revenue swelling the Anfield coffers is the club's share of income generated from the Premier League renegotiation of Sky's live cable and satellite television rights. Liverpool also stand to profit from ITV's Premiership highlights and Champions League package. The club's rising profile in both meant they benefited to the tune of some £18 million in the 2000–01 season from the sale of Premiership television rights (including a merit share, worth approximately £6 million as a reward for coming third in the league, and another £6 million from appearance bonus money, as Liverpool were one of the two most televised teams). More recently, qualification for the Second Phase of the Champions League alone in the 2001–02 campaign guaranteed the Reds a further £20 million.

The biannual change of the home strip has been supplemented, in the past few years, by annual changes of the away kit and, in 2001, the introduction of a special home kit exclusively designed to 'commemorate' Liverpool's return to Europe's premier competition, the Champions League. Frequent strip changes are a major bone of contention for supporters' clubs. However, the new European shirt did, at least, promote the club's Liver Bird emblem above the shirt sponsor's name, which was a welcome development and one reflective of Liverpool's continued struggle to balance the forces of commercialisation with maintaining the rich tradition of the club (although the club's tinkering with the emblem on the new 2002–03 home kit has not been so well received by the die-hards).

Despite the board's best efforts, there remains criticism of the direction the club is heading in, with some fans concerned, in the wake of the Treble success and its relentless marketing by the club, that Liverpool might be on the threshold of emulating Manchester United off as well as on the pitch. United, with their self-styled 'theatre of dreams' symbolism, circus-like stadium announcements, public flirtation with Rupert Murdoch's News International/BSkyB empire, endless kit changes and overblown marketing campaigns have always been given very short shrift by Liverpool supporters, who feel United is run more as a business than a football club. But however unpalatable the consequences, the hard truth remains that Liverpool need to be able to compete with United on commercial terms if they are to match their achievements on the playing field. The answer – and the Liverpool board are acutely aware of this – lies in doing so without sacrificing the club's soul. As Rick Parry remarked whilst discussing the possibility of sponsors putting their names to stands at the club's proposed new ground: 'We're going to keep our heritage to ourselves. We're not believers in selling our birthright.'

And while supporters may be nervous at seeing their club move so brazenly into the commercial mainstream, the upside to this new display of business acumen is millions of pounds raised from the likes of Granada and Reebok for reinvesting in the club's most valuable asset, its playing staff, whether through bankrolling Houllier's transfer policy, or developing the Academy to nurture the Owens, Fowlers and McManamans of the next generation. Without that injection of capital, Liverpool would not be able to boast Europe's best-equipped youth academy. Located in Kirkby, North Liverpool, it boasts state-of-the-art indoor pitches where the surface is designed to act exactly like grass, even to the extent of allowing slide challenges to be made without risk of injury. It may have been built at a cost of £12 million, but the outlay needs to be seen in context. Steven Gerrard is a product of the Academy and already, even at a conservative estimate, worth at least twice the amount it cost to build. While it could be argued that someone of Gerrard's talent would have made the grade had he been forced to train on the remains of an Iron Age hill-fort, the presence of outstanding facilities at Liverpool, such as the Academy and the high-tech training complex at Melwood, will continue to play a vital role in attracting the cream of local young talent to the club, thus preventing it from signing for Liverpool's rivals further down the East Lancs Road.

Melwood, Liverpool's traditional first-team training ground, was overhauled twice in the late '90s to become an impressive, pioneering fusion of computer-controlled gymnasia and full-size training pitches, including an all-weather synthetic surface and two pitches relaid in 1999 to the quality of the turf at Anfield. The computerised gym equipment enables more accurate monitoring of players' fitness levels, as each player is given his own key card to store his performance data. Melwood also features a sauna, specialist rehabilitation rooms and a hydrotherapy pool. At Houllier's insistence, the rehabilitation area is deliberately on a balcony overlooking the open-plan fitness centre so that the injured players can be inspired by their team mates. The main dressing-room has a curved wall to help create a feeling of unity and togetherness.

The sophistication of the club's modern training facilities is mirrored by a scientific and carefully thought-out approach to every aspect of the players' development and match preparation. From his first season at Anfield, Gérard Houllier has sought to ensure the provision of specialist staff to provide classes on health, fitness, diet and nutrition for the players. After training, for example, the squad sit down to a light lunch (no dairy products, although red wine is optional). Much of the teaching is based on ideas Houllier developed at the French national academy.

Houllier is also responsible for an innovative approach to the problems posed by travelling away from home in European competition. Unlike many of their Premiership rivals, Liverpool prefer to stay the night in the city after the tie is played – whether it is Kiev, Istanbul or Barcelona. This enables the players to undergo a thorough warm-down session and get a good night's sleep in a hotel they are already familiar with. The team will return the following day in leisurely fashion, even though they may have a league game just forty-eight hours later. The results have been startling: in the 2001–02 season, Liverpool picked up a remarkable 34 points from a possible 36 after Champions League matches, compared to Manchester United's paltry haul of just 14 from the same number of fixtures. United took the more orthodox route of flying straight back after an away game to ensure the players could get a full training session in the following day. Houllier sets great store by getting the groundwork absolutely right, to the extent of taking a hands-on role in each area of match preparation. Even while recuperating from open-heart surgery, he found time to travel to Istanbul to check on facilities ahead of an important Champions League fixture against Galatasaray.

The modernisation of Liverpool as a force capable of competing with Europe's top tier of clubs is almost complete. Developing Melwood and the Academy has not been a contentious or difficult task; expanding into new media streams was a logical and natural step forward; identifying and then working with the right commercial partners to build the club's brand has been achieved with a minimum of fuss; the implementation of new and imaginative approaches to training, travel arrangements and every detail of match preparation has, under Gérard Houllier's expert guidance, been quick and successful. The ethos of a winning team supported by a well-oiled infrastructure is now integrated into the club's philosophy. In each of these areas, modern Liverpool is a club at the forefront of the game's superpowers. But, in one key area, Liverpool still lags behind its rivals: its stadium is too small.

For the past four years, the biggest dilemma facing Rick Parry and the Liverpool board, as the club seeks to match the spending power of Europe's elite, has been how best to approach the issue of increasing ground capacity. Anfield's 45,000 ceiling is simply not big enough, given there are currently over 10,000 people on the waiting list for season tickets alone. When compared to Barcelona's 110,000 capacity at the Nou Camp, or even Old Trafford's 67,500, this figure appears trifling. It is undoubtedly a constraint on Liverpool's ability to maximise revenue from ticket receipts and, in consequence, enable the club to plough money back into building a team capable of making Liverpool a major force in Europe. But, as the board weigh up the options in going forward, the club must ask itself an important question: to what extent is it right for the club to try and compete with the inflated salaries paid to the biggest stars on the continent? There are surely salient lessons to be learnt from the decline in profitability in Italian football. *Serie A* matches are now regularly played in front of huge, half-empty concrete stadia. Clubs with the pedigree of AC Milan, Lazio and Fiorentina are facing mounting debt and, recently, Rangers' chairman, David Murray predicted that the day when a major European club goes into liquidation is fast approaching. Silvio Berlusconi, AC Milan's chairman, is so concerned about falling attendances and the damage this will do to the television spectacle, that he can now envisage a time when fans are let in for nothing.

If the 2001–02 season is anything to go by, football's long-sustained boom period has finally reached the end of the road. If the game is not careful, the hot air that has kept the boom afloat will quickly be followed by cold feet, of the variety already displayed by ITV Digital, which last season first sought to re-negotiate their £300 million deal with the Football League (after dismally low viewing figures led to an advertising take-up more akin to a late-night episode of *Prisoner Cell Block H*), only to go into administration after the League refused to play ball. The reality is that football on television has reached saturation point, advertising revenues have hit a downturn and new technologies like broadband have been slow to roll out. The crippling cost of paying vast salaries and building new stadia can no longer be supported by income from media coverage of the game – even, possibly, in its highest echelons. Liverpool's wage bill constituted a staggering 75 per cent of the club's turnover for the 1999–2000 season.

Liverpool are not immune to these problems and, in the current climate, the board are wise to think carefully about their proposed stadium redevelopment. While Premier League games routinely sell out, attendance at domestic cup games and even during the first phase of the Champions League have not always been great. The Liverpool v. Boavista match, which marked the Reds' long-awaited return to Europe's premier competition, was seen by a crowd some 10,000 short of capacity. Admittedly, it was played on the evening of September 11 but, nonetheless, one would have expected such a momentous occasion to have sold out in advance.

Football is also not just about the economics of crowd figures. Atmosphere and the maintenance of tradition are critical factors in a club's well-being, particularly a club with the rich heritage of Liverpool. Anfield may be some 20,000 short of Old Trafford's capacity, but its position as Britain's most famous and distinguished stadium is unrivalled. On the big European nights, such as the memorable UEFA Cup semi-final victory over Barcelona, or Gérard Houllier's emotional return to the fray for the decisive Champions League encounter with Roma, there is no better arena to exploit the raw passion and drama of the occasion. Even Sven-Goran

Eriksson, not someone you would think of as an ambience-chaser, was moved to admit that the Kop in full voice belting out 'You'll Never Walk Alone' made the hairs stand up on the back of his neck.

But, given that the board feel there is no option but to increase ground capacity (even if they were to adopt a more cautious outlook on the future of football's popularity and aim for 55,000 rather than 70,000), the question is how to go about doing so. It comes down to a straight choice: stay at Anfield and expand, or move to a new site and build a stadium from scratch. In April 2002, after years of consultation and planning, the club finally announced that they had opted to move to a new 55,000-seater stadium at Stanley Park. The proposed move has been fraught with complications from the outset and has polarised opinion among the club's supporters, many of whom feel it is fundamental to Liverpool's identity to remain at Anfield. Perhaps the decision to leave should not come as a surprise, but it has been hard to keep track of all the to-ing and fro-ing.

Initially, when the plans for redevelopment were in their infancy, all the signs pointed towards a move to a new stadium. The board always had their sights firmly set on remaining in north Liverpool, where the emotional bond that links the club to its supporters is at its most intense. Stanley Park was quickly targeted as the obvious location for rebuilding. However, to add to the confusion, the club had to demonstrate that the planning process had been done thoroughly, so alternative sites, including edge-of-town areas like Speke, were examined (however cursorily). At first, the option of redeveloping Anfield was given short shrift, Rick Parry stating: 'I just don't see that happening, because that's what the community objected to most of all. You can't do that without the demolition of about 250 houses.'

Yet, Stanley Park was hardly a straightforward option, given the cost and time that would need to be expended in developing a brand-new stadium. The club's ability to build on Stanley Park in the near future is heavily dependent on the community's support for the project and, by the end of 2001, an 18-month public consultation with local residents and businesses showed people remained divided over whether they wanted to see the new ground developed on the existing site or moved to the park. Such a response highlights the risk of significant objection to a Stanley Park planning application and, with it, a public inquiry which would add at least 12 months to the process, with no assurance as to the eventual outcome. In addition, English Heritage has also raised concerns over proposals to build the new stadium at Stanley Park. Once the uncertainty as to raising the necessary finance is added into the equation (and Liverpool would need to benefit from the kind of public sector grant that Everton's Kings Arena plan will enjoy), Stanley Park begins to look an increasingly unrealistic option – at least in its prototype 70,000 capacity – despite Rick Parry's plea that a move to the area would form part of a comprehensive regeneration plan.

In fact, once the board had set their sights on a lower capacity after it became apparent that the '90s football boom was drawing to a close, the less costly redevelopment of the existing ground at Anfield became – for a time – the club's preferred option (the board publicly acknowledged as much as late as January 2002). What ultimately scuppered the prospect of staying at Anfield was the impracticality of expanding the Main Stand. Although the club are in a position to extend the Anfield Road end, as they own all the properties in the adjoining road and have been told by the council that closing the road will not be an issue, this will only increase the capacity by a further 4,500. For the reconstruction of Anfield to be viable, the Main Stand needs to be completely rebuilt and this will entail the demolition of up to three streets running parallel to it and the destruction of over 200 houses. This is feasible, although obtaining the necessary Compulsory Purchase Orders would hinge on Liverpool City Council, which, to date, has been either reluctant or unwilling to make any decision. Even with the council's support, the disruption caused to the club by rebuilding the Main Stand would be considerable. As Rick Parry explained: 'It would be a much bigger job than rebuilding the Kop because of all the facilities and the dressing-rooms within the Main Stand. We would have to considerably reduce the capacity within the stadium for a long period of time. Also, when we were building the new Kop we weren't playing European football and there weren't as many midweek games as there are today. It was a case back then of the builders doing the work during the week and then handing the stadium back to us for weekend games. That just wouldn't be possible today.'

Whichever route they opted for, the club would have been guilty of extreme optimism at best and hubris at worse had they decided to press on with their plans for an Old Trafford-sized arena in the wake of the ITV Digital farrago. The board has always stressed that the club will not go ahead with a stadium-building scheme to the detriment of team building. Success on the pitch must always remain the priority; Liverpool cannot afford to get into a situation where the club is paying so much for the stadium that it cannot support the team. Yet, having made the decision to move to a new site, Liverpool are now caught in a Catch-22. Why build something that can only hold 55,000 people when the income generated by, say, 65,000 would put the Reds on a par with Manchester United? Parry outlined the dilemma thus: 'Capacity is something we've looked at with great care; it's not about vanity. It's about planning for success and not for mediocrity. You've got to assume we'll get back to the glory days, and although you can't guarantee that we're going to fill it if we're not succeeding, if we haven't got the capacity will we ever succeed?'

The delay in reaching a decision on the ground's future has probably not harmed the club over much. In football's present uncertain climate, Liverpool are fortunate they did not commit to a multi-million pound venture that could ultimately prove a hostage to fortune and a spoke in the wheels of Gérard Houllier's best-laid team-building plans. Although the new stadium will cost up to £70 million to build and will not be ready until the start of the 2005 season, the original blueprint had a projected cost of £120 million. It is a great shame to see the club departing their original home but the new ground will still be called Anfield, and will be only 300 yards away from its current site. With the incorporation of key Anfield landmarks such as the Hillsborough memorial and the Shankly and Paisley Gates in the new design, the signs are positive that Liverpool's new stadium will do justice to the original. It certainly has a lot to live up to.

9

The Reds in Europe

The past is weighing on the players' shoulders. To make a name for themselves in Europe. I would be so happy, so happy for the boys.

Gérard Houllier

Of the many legacies handed down by Bill Shankly, the creation of a team capable of challenging the pre-eminence of Europe's great sides – Real Madrid, Juventus and Cruyff's Ajax – was perhaps the most important. Shankly laid the foundations; Paisley drew on the work of Liverpool's greatest architect to build the most dominant force in European football since the legendary Real Madrid sides of the 1960s won five European Cups in successive seasons.

Liverpool's great nights of European glory are etched in the minds of the club's (older) supporters: Keegan's valedictory bow in perhaps the greatest triumph of them all – 1977's first European Cup victory; the conquest of St Etienne en route to that final; Dalglish's adroit finish at Wembley a year later to retain the trophy; Cruyff's Anfield master-class of 1967; Grobbelaar's penalty shoot-out antics in Rome, and the destruction of Inter Milan in 1965, during Liverpool's first season of European football.

It was nights like those that the Liverpool faithful pined for during the impoverished years of the '90s under Souness and Evans. The great Liverpool sides had built their reputation on their ability to play the 'European way', a progressive, fluid style based on patient passing and careful probing for openings, particularly away from home, where the Reds were content to slow the pace down and squeeze the life out of the game.

At Anfield, the team were remorseless, launching wave after wave of attacks on the opposition goal. Home or away, the emphasis was on keeping possession. Liverpool, masters of that particular art throughout their 15-year hegemony in England, used their success in Europe to build on their supremacy in the domestic game. The Reds were always at least one step ahead of their nearest rivals, their football capable of a sophistication and tactical appreciation beyond their English challengers, acquired from years of pitting their wits against Europe's finest. The six-year ban from competing in Europe that followed the Heysel tragedy of 1985 first undermined and then eroded Liverpool's dominance in England. The turbulent end to Dalglish's reign laid bare the fissures running through the club. By the early '90s, the Reds were out of touch with the currents of European football and no longer able to attract big-name players. For the club's younger supporters, European competition was variously a hazy memory, the province of a video collection or, worse still, under first Souness and then Evans, the source of considerable embarrassment. The restoration of Liverpool's fortunes in Europe was therefore critical if the team were to regain their superiority at home. In Gérard Houllier, Liverpool had a manager not only conscious of that legacy, but dedicated to re-establishing his team as a powerful force, revered across the continent.

2000–2001 SEASON

After the false start of the Evans–Houllier alliance and subsequent failure to qualify for European competition in the following season, Liverpool's first game in Europe under Houllier's sole leadership did not take place until September 2000. The team had secured a place in the UEFA Cup, now much reduced in status as the Champions League poorer cousin. Nonetheless, with the former Cup-winners' Cup amalgamated into the UEFA Cup and the tournament retaining its knock-out status (rather than affording the luxury of being able to lose games in the group stages and still qualify for the next round), Liverpool's re-entry into Europe provided a demanding new assignment for Houllier's players. A trip to the Romanian capital to face Rapid Bucharest in the opening round emphasised the quality of the opposition. In later rounds, Houllier's victorious team were to come up against Porto, Barcelona and Roma.

Gérard Houllier's approach to European ties was not radically different to his preparation for the more earthy demands of the Premiership. Initially, the main tactical departure was the deployment of a lone striker for away matches in a 4-5-1 formation; in other words, the Premiership's counter-attacking policy, only more so. Scoring an away goal or two still retained its importance in the two-legged knock-out, however, so this system required some adventurous support play from the attacking midfielders. Houllier will have been pleased, therefore, with Nick Barmby's first goal since his move across Stanley Park, after a penetrative run by Owen, as the Reds secured an impressive first-leg advantage in Bucharest. It mattered not that the return at Anfield was a dour affair, with caution hindering Liverpool's approach as they maintained a defensive shape throughout, protecting their slender lead. The UEFA Cup run continued in similar vein through the next two rounds, the Reds proving difficult to break down, particularly at home.

Having overcome the Greeks of Olympiakos with their best performance to date, a stylishly conceived 2–0 victory at Anfield in early December, Liverpool were handed, as their reward, the tie that Houllier craved most: an opportunity to test his embryonic team against one of Europe's leading lights. Roma were to be Liverpool's barrier to a place in the quarter-finals of the competition. After years of pitting their wits against modest or unglamorous opposition in Europe, it felt like the Reds had finally arrived back in the big time (prior to Roma, Liverpool's most celebrated European exploit in the preceding 15 years had been overturning a two-goal deficit against little-known French outfit Auxerre). The anticipation alone of resuming battle with the side vanquished in Liverpool's last European Cup triumph in 1984 brought an added dimension to the Reds' season, although few fans could have envisaged the extraordinary scenes that would accompany a memorable first-leg triumph in Italy's capital.

By winning in Rome's Stadio Olympico (the scene of two of Liverpool's previous European Cup triumphs), the Reds regained their position as a member of European football's elite. And they did so in some style, turning in a vintage exhibition of controlled, counter-attacking football which exposed the *Serie A* leaders' limitations in the absence of the injured Francesco Totti. Liverpool, too, had absentees of their own – most notably Gerrard – as they lined up, not in their customary 4-5-1 away European formation, but with two strikers – pairing Fowler and Owen in attack from the outset for only the third time all season. After a tense opening 20 minutes, when Roma's slick passing unsettled Liverpool, the first half settled into an enjoyably uneventful affair, following the pattern of dogged defending and intermittent forays into the opposition half which had characterised the Reds' UEFA Cup performances throughout the season. Roma were restricted to just one clear opening – a header by Delvecchio, which flew narrowly wide in first-half stoppage-time. Hyypiä otherwise kept a tight rein on the Roma striker, denying him the time or space to link Roma's forward play.

The second period began explosively. Rinaldi attempted a dangerous square-pass across the edge of his own penalty area; Owen, sensing his intentions, reacted sharply and intercepted before drawing goalkeeper Antonioli and placing the ball clinically into the corner of the net. The goal took a second to sink in; Owen's elation, a mixture of relief and joy, confirmed that Liverpool were indeed 1–0 up in the Stadio Olympico. Visibly lifted by taking the lead, Liverpool moved forward with renewed purpose, Hamann – in his best Liverpool performance to date – breaking up Roma's attacks and launching Liverpool's counter-thrusts in the same movement. A sharp one-two between Ziege and Hyypiä gave the German a chance to clip in a cross from Roma's left. Owen, darting to the near-post, met the ball with a deft flick of the head, and Liverpool had the breathing space of a two-goal advantage.

Roma worked hard to gain a foothold in the tie, but appeared stunned by Owen's double strike. Liverpool looked the more likely to score, Barmby shooting straight at Antonioli when clean through. A third goal would have been more than Houllier could have dreamed of, and there was no hiding his delight at the final whistle. 'The whole team was superb,' he cried. 'For the first time in as long as I can remember, I felt like pouring myself a beer and just reflecting on what I'd seen. Our composure and attitude were so good and I couldn't have asked for more in terms of striking the right blend between attack and defence.'

The plaudits were fully deserved, but could not disguise the fact that Liverpool still had a fair way to travel before they would be able to compete not merely as gatecrashers at the exclusive Champions League party, but as equals to Europe's blue-bloods. The return leg demonstrated that a gulf in class still existed, as Roma's superior passing and ball retention at times embarrassed the home team. Later in the campaign, Houllier reflected on the extent of the examination posed by footballing technicians of the calibre of Totti, Batistuta and Cafu: 'I still think Roma, especially, were better than us,' Houllier admitted. 'Michael Owen made a huge difference in the first leg, but when you are playing a team of such quality, one with more European experience than you have, you have to try to be more clever.' Liverpool survived Roma's second-leg bombardment by a combination of good fortune, resolute defending and – as Houllier surmised – an intelligent approach to the task in hand (manifested in the tactical discipline of the performance more than its technical expertise) to claim a place in the last eight against Porto.

Already, in reaching the quarter-finals, Liverpool had surpassed pre-season expectations and given their supporters cause for guarded optimism about the prospects of winning their first European trophy in 17 years. The manner in which a technically proficient Porto were brushed aside raised the anticipation to fever-pitch level. After a thoroughly professional hatchet job in Portugal (the Reds grinding out another thrill-free 0–0), Liverpool turned up the heat at Anfield, running out 2–0 winners in a game notable for the return to peak form of Michael Owen. With Owen firing on all cylinders, anything was possible.

Suddenly, and without having extended themselves unduly (save for the home leg against Roma), Liverpool were in the semi-finals of a major European competition and journeying to the Iberian peninsula once more for a showdown with Rivaldo's Barcelona. The game was the most sterile of goalless draws, as Liverpool drew the sting from Barça's attack. Houllier was naturally satisfied with his charges' ability to disrupt the home team's rhythm: 'Barcelona's strength is in their attacking play and if you let them play they are likely to tear you apart. We knew we could frustrate them. I make no apologies for going out and doing that in the first leg. There is nothing in the rules that says teams going to the Nou Camp have got to make it easy for Barcelona.' As against Roma two rounds earlier, Liverpool eventually triumphed against opponents better equipped than they for European conflict, through the astute planning of their manager and the vigilance with which the players carried out Houllier's tactical plans. Barcelona failed to breach the Reds' defence in either match, failing to score in both legs of a European tie for the first time in over 20 years. Barça's coach Ferrer conceded that his side had been outmanoeuvred by his counterpart's gameplan: 'Liverpool defended well in both ties and in the second half they broke up the play very well, and we were forced to hit long balls which we are not used to.'

Liverpool's resilience and discipline, allied to strong defence and spells of fine attacking play, had ensured a safe passage to their first European final in 16 years. While such an achievement had been a focused team effort, the performance of three individuals stood out: Hamann's intelligent shielding of the back four, Hyypiä's commanding presence at the heart of the defence and Owen's predatory finishing were the platform upon which Liverpool's success had been built. Now, these players, along with their colleagues, faced the ultimate challenge: writing their names in the annals of Liverpool FC as victors in Europe. Houllier suggested that victory could herald a new era for the Reds and told his players they were playing for 'a place in history'.

UEFA CUP FINAL: LIVERPOOL 5 ALAVÉS 4

'I think it will be a low-scoring game.'
Jordi Cruyff, Alavés, the day before the final

The build-up to the final was complicated by Liverpool's domestic cup commitments. Four days before the clash of footballing cultures with Spanish unknowns Alavés in Dortmund, the Reds came from behind to overcome Arsenal in the energy-sapping heat of the Millennium Stadium to claim the FA Cup. In the aftermath of victory, Houllier concentrated on focusing his players' minds and asked them to dig deeper still into their physical reserves. Alavés were in the UEFA Cup final on merit and sensed that this was their moment; Liverpool would have to perform at, or close to, their peak to prevail.

The final could not have been scripted (except by a higher power with a taste for the absurd); the game was dramatically played out to an audience at once enthralled and bemused by the events unfolding before them. Against all expectations, both teams attacked in cavalier fashion, each seemingly hell-bent on trying to outdo the other in the number of men they were prepared to commit to attack. Liverpool stormed into a two-goal lead inside 15 minutes. Alavés, on their first appearance in a European Cup final, froze, with their passes frequently going astray and their tackles mistimed. Gerrard and Hamann assumed control of the midfield, while McAllister exploited the gaps in the Spanish defence with precision. Alavés coach Jose-Manuel Esnal made a bold early substitution, sending on forward Ivan Alonso in the place of a shell-shocked defender. His gamble quickly paid off: Alonso succeeded in unsettling Hyypiä and Henchoz and brought Alavés back into the match with a well-taken header. But by half-time Liverpool had reasserted their authority and McAllister's coolly converted penalty, after Owen was sent tumbling by Alavés' reckless goalkeeper, restored their two-goal advantage.

In the sanctuary of the dressing-room, Liverpool prepared themselves for a renewed onslaught from their opponents. The trade in cheap goals duly resumed, as Alavés, incredibly, hauled themselves level within five minutes of the re-start, La Liga's leading scorer, Javi Moreno, scoring twice in the blink of an eye. The score in the final that was confidently predicted to be a dismal goalless draw now stood at 3–3. And the drama was only just beginning. Having tormented Liverpool's defenders all evening, Moreno was now promptly – and bafflingly – substituted. Reds' supporters breathed a collective sigh of relief and then raised the volume to deafening heights as their hero prepared to make his entrance, with the words of his manager driving him to score. Fowler's emergence from the bench to finesse a right-footed shot into the corner of the net after being played in by a slide-rule McAllister pass only added to the sense of wonderment which now percolated through the stadium. McAllister was living up to the occasion, rapidly becoming the epicentre around which a remarkable football match ebbed and flowed (a grateful Houllier later suggested 'the only mistake McAllister has made in his career is not signing for us earlier').

Ordinarily, Fowler's goal would have proved the fairytale winner but, in the topsy-turvy parallel universe of the Westfalen Stadion, there was to be a sting in this particular fairytale: Cruyff headed home a corner in the 93rd minute to take the match into extra-time. The usually dependable Henchoz ('he was sinking out there', Houllier later said) was withdrawn in favour of Smicer, and Owen departed to be replaced by Berger, as Houllier introduced a Czech flavour to proceedings. Somehow Houllier's troops rallied from the disappointment of conceding a last-minute equaliser to dominate extra-time. Alavés lost two men to reckless challenges in the final 30 minutes, the second on Smicer resulting in the golden goal winner, as McAllister's free kick was unwittingly headed into his own net by Geli, with a penalty shoot-out beckoning. The supporters' frayed nerves could not have withstood such drama. After the jubilant Sami Hyypiä and Robbie Fowler had held aloft Liverpool's third pot of the season, Houllier was quick to pay tribute to the most exacting of adversaries: 'I thought Alavés were brilliant. It takes two sides to make a great final and I liked the way they showed the same resilience and determination as us. They looked dangerous every time they got the ball.' The narrowest of victories was celebrated in expansive fashion on the pitch amidst a sea of red and blue tickertape (both teams' colours admittedly, but then the final was in Germany, so efficiency in the presentation ceremony did not come as a surprise). The intensity of the supporters' emotions made for a moving scene. 'Standing in a big huddle, with the staff and the players in front of the Liverpool fans at the end, reminded me of the Shankly era,' Houllier said. 'But I am embarrassed by comparisons with the team of the past. There will never be a team like that.'

Liverpool would not be defending their trophy, however: three days after lifting the UEFA Cup to scenes of unrestrained joy and a rousing reception from both sets of supporters (the sportsmanship and camaraderie displayed by both clubs' fans was publicly praised by UEFA), the Reds secured a top-three finish in the Premiership with a last-day victory at Charlton. The result meant that next year Liverpool would be embarking, at long last, on their first Champions League campaign.

2001–02 SEASON

Liverpool made their reacquaintance with Europe's foremost competition in eerily similar circumstances to those in which they took their leave 17 years before – to a backdrop of human tragedy. This time, the situation was not connected to the club, as Liverpool's opening group match against Boavista went ahead under the pall of the events of September 11. Understandably, the game was played in a subdued atmosphere and a 1–1 draw, salvaged by a fine Owen goal, constituted a reasonable start.

By the time of the side's trip to Kiev for a critical fixture at the halfway stage in the group, Liverpool had been rocked back by the loss of Houllier, their leader and prime European strategist. At this point, qualification for the second phase seemed a remote possibility. But the Reds gritted it out and emerged triumphant, thanks to goals by Murphy and Gerrard. This second successive victory over Dynamo Kiev (following on from the Litmanen-inspired victory in the home tie a fortnight earlier) paved the way for a place in the last 16. Qualification was assured against Borussia Dortmund in the first game to be played at Anfield since Houllier had been driven from the ground in an ambulance, complaining of chest pains. The atmosphere now was in marked contrast to that which ushered in the campaign on September 11, as Smicer volleyed the Reds in front barely ten minutes in, presaging a vibrant display of controlled possession football.

While Liverpool's ability to see off the challenge of Dynamo Kiev and Borussia Dortmund signified they were ready to acquit themselves in the Champions League, they must have thought the first phase was a kindergarten, if the lessons handed out by Barcelona in the opening match of the second round were anything to go by. Still, a demoralising 3–1 defeat could not eclipse the fact that for an hour or so, the Reds had been the better team. Had Owen not uncharacteristically missed an open goal with the score at 1–1, the game would probably have taken a different course. As it was, the defeat was followed by no fewer than four consecutive draws (including three nil–nils – count 'em). However, in a very tight group, Liverpool, despite having failed to register a win thus far, approached their final group fixture in the peculiar position of knowing a victory against Roma would almost certainly guarantee a quarter-final place.

Unlike the Giallorossis' visit to Anfield at the same stage in the previous season when Roma arrived with more than one eye on clinching the *Scudetto*, no one could doubt the authenticity of the challenge that awaited the Reds this time round. But Liverpool had a trick up their sleeve – Gérard Houllier, with a taste for the dramatically opportune, chose the moment of reckoning for Liverpool's European aspirations to stage his remarkable comeback from illness. As the players assembled for a final pre-match briefing shortly before 6 p.m. at their hotel on the Albert Dock, Gérard surprised them by turning up to deliver the team talk. 'I think tonight is going to be a special night and I wanted to be with you,' Houllier told them. 'When he got on the bus to go to the game you could tell the players were lifted. It made for a magical night. I just knew we wouldn't be beaten. You could feel the passion rolling around the stadium,' recounted Phil Thompson afterwards. Suitably inspired, the Reds laid siege to their opponents' goal and, after a pulsating opening 20 minutes, the outcome of the tie was firmly in Liverpool's hands. Litmanen's early penalty was supplemented by an athletic leap of grace and power by Heskey, who buried his header into the Kop goal to condemn the Italians to defeat. The Reds had emerged from the most evenly contested of groups, with their parsimonious defence breached just once in five matches since the opening-round fixture against Barcelona, to clinch the second qualifying place.

Alas, the adventure could not last. Liverpool came unstuck in the quarter-finals against the underrated German side, Bayer Leverkusen. Leading 1–0 after a tense and disjointed first-leg, the Reds' rearguard was surprisingly pierced on four occasions in an open return at the Bay Arena, as Leverkusen's quick, skilful attackers pulled Liverpool's defenders this way and that, the Brazilian winger Ze Roberto giving Xavier a torrid time. Even the normally unflappable Dudek appeared ruffled and made what most observers counted as his first mistake in six months' safe custody of Liverpool's goal – failing to keep out Ballack's well struck, but routine, drive. After the thrill of Roma, the sense of disappointment was palpable. Houllier had gone on record before the match as believing his team were 'ten games from greatness', implying that if all ten were won, the Premiership and the European Cup would be Liverpool's. It was not to be and Houllier, who normally chose his public pronouncements with such deliberation, appeared a little premature in proclaiming his side's virtues.

Leverkusen also served to highlight the tactical paradox at the heart of Liverpool's revival under Houllier: the quest for a successful balance between defence and attack without compromising one for the other. This dilemma was epitomised by Houllier's difficulties in integrating Jari Litmanen into his meticulously conceived team pattern, at the expense of Emile Heskey – a more team-minded, but arguably less creative-forward. It was a conundrum which Houllier had failed to solve thus far, partly because of his team's shortcomings at this stage in their development. Against the best opposition, Liverpool struggled to retain possession, but remained hard to break down, with Heskey (sardonically portrayed as a 'defender operating in enemy territory' by *El Pais*) working tirelessly to pressure the opposition centre-halves and thus helping to strangle attacks at birth. Forty minutes into the second leg at the Bay Arena and Heskey, having recently jetted back from the Caribbean after a family bereavement, pulled up with a tight hamstring. The Reds were trailing 1–0, but had weathered the early storm. Litmanen's introduction, as Heskey's replacement, brought about a noticeable weakening in Liverpool's ability to defend from the front. The team were overrun in midfield throughout the second half, as Litmanen struggled to impose himself. Nonetheless, he still conjured up a brilliant goal out of nothing which took his side to within five minutes of a Champions League semi-final. And nor should Litmanen's defensive limitations be seen as the sole cause of Leverkusen's second-half dominance. Hamann and Gerrard were both out of sorts: the main flaw in Gerrard's game at this point in his career – an occasional lack of composure on the ball and in his decision making – was painfully exposed by the magnificent Ballack.

After the game, Houllier was roundly chastised for making a tactical error in substituting Hamann with an hour gone and the score 1–1. Yet, Liverpool were already swamped in midfield and the thinking behind the change (in which the more attack-minded Smicer replaced the German) was to try and switch the emphasis and force Leverkusen onto the back foot. The plan did not work, because Smicer made no impact and the team as a whole continued to surrender possession too cheaply. But Hamann's withdrawal also pinpointed another deficiency in Houllier's Liverpool: the squad may have been one of the largest in the Premiership, but too many of its understudies failed to provide an adequate alternative to the leading men. In this case, Houllier's central midfield options in Leverkusen amounted to the 37-year-old McAllister and Igor Biscan who, after a promising start, had not impressed in his rare outings in the first-team.

Although Liverpool had failed in their quest for a fifth European Cup, to get within touching distance of the semi-finals of the Champions League in their first campaign was still a notable achievement. It had taken Alex Ferguson's Manchester United five years to reach the same level and Arsenal, for all their domestic success under Wenger, had still gone no further than one quarter-final appearance in four attempts. Liverpool had played 14 Champions League matches and lost just two, although they had managed only 14 goals, a return that reflected the side's defensive outlook in the majority of these games.

Still, there were several positives to come out of the club's first experience of competing at the highest level of European football since the Heysel tragedy of 1985. The tactical and defensive disciplines which stood them in good stead throughout their concurrent Premiership campaign, withstood the toughest of examinations from Europe's best strikers: goalless draws in Rome, Barcelona and Dortmund were ample testimony to that. Going forward, Liverpool had, at times, reached, although rarely sustained, an impressive level of incisive, attacking football: Murphy's passing in Istanbul stands out, alongside the quality of some passages of the team's play during that most unforgiving of European assignments, Dynamo Kiev in the Ukraine. Above all, the verve and aggression of their dismantling of Roma's thoroughbreds showed what Houllier's Liverpool were capable of at their peak. That such a supercharged performance owed much to Houllier's shock return to the touchline can be counter-balanced by the fact that Liverpool delivered without two key players – Owen and Hamann.

Weighed against the considerable sense of anti-climax precipitated by the Reds' sudden collapse at the Bay Arena, Liverpool's only two defeats were against Barcelona, who reached the semi-finals, and Bayer Leverkusen, who disposed of Manchester United en route to the final. In other words, Liverpool had fought against and frequently succeeded in holding their own with the aristocrats of European football in their debut Champions League campaign. As Gérard Houllier retreated to the Bunker to plot the next stage of his squad-rebuilding ahead of his fourth season in sole charge, he did so in the knowledge that his young team stood, if not on the threshold, at least a good deal nearer to winning Europe's most coveted prize than just 12 months previously.

10

The Houllier Crisis: Liverpool Fight Back
(2001–02 Season)

It hadn't made for comfortable viewing: the team were playing badly and were deservedly losing to a rampant Leeds. Liverpool were a goal down, but it could have been worse after a listless first-half showing. Heskey, who had been ineffectual thus far, was in the treatment room with the club doctor Mark Waller, struggling to overcome a knee injury. Gérard Houllier signalled to Vladimir Smicer and Jari Litmanen to begin warming up and called his assistant, Phil Thompson, over: 'Listen, the first half was poor. Leave the start of the team-talk to me. I will make one or two changes.' Houllier later recalled, with some relief, the next few, life-changing moments that led to his sudden and premature departure from the ground. Struggling to summon the energy to address his team, he had managed a few words of encouragement, but the pains in his chest wouldn't go away. Hiding his discomfort from his players, Houllier cut short his team-talk and left the sanctuary of the dressing-room, heading for the treatment area to speak to the doctor.

He felt suddenly worse, but the pain was not unbearable. In the treatment room Mark Waller was still working with Heskey. Houllier managed to joke, 'Don't worry. He is worth more money than me, but I am more urgent!' But his distress was obvious. 'As the team doctor looked at me, Emile was peering up with worried eyes at what was going on. He has since told one of my friends that he did not sleep that night.' The doctor took Gérard's blood pressure and his reaction was instant. He summoned an ambulance and told a colleague to call Gérard's wife Isabelle and friend

Norman Gard, who were sitting together in the Main Stand. Houllier was still convinced he would be watching the second half of the game and asked when he could go back to the dug-out. He was told in no uncertain terms that he had seen the last of the match. As the second half kicked off, Gérard Houllier, breathing through an oxygen mask, was being driven in a paramedic ambulance to the Liverpool NHS Trust's Cardiothoracic Centre at Broadgreen. On his arrival, Houllier, still unaware of the seriousness of his condition, appeared more concerned for his team, asking for the latest score and who had scored the equaliser.

Back at Anfield, as the players trudged wearily back to the dressing-room having salvaged a draw, they were informed that their manager had been rushed to hospital. They showered and changed; one or two managed perfunctory post-match interviews, and then they were gone – back to their homes, to await further news of their boss and mentor. A six-hour flight to the Ukranian capital, Kiev, loomed uncomfortably on the horizon. Would Gérard be flying out with them?

As they would soon discover, the answer was an unequivocal 'no'. Their manager lay unconscious on the operating table at Broadgreen's Cardiothoracic Centre, in the middle of 14-hour surgery to repair a dissected aorta, the artery that pumps newly oxygenated blood from the heart. Gérard Houllier's condition was life threatening and had required immediate surgery, a diagnosis that Gérard had only become aware of at the last possible moment. The procedure turned out to be a lot more complicated than the specialists had anticipated because the leak had been happening for a long time. Fortunately, the Broadgreen medical team were able to repair the aorta and keep Gérard stable, though still unconscious, on a respirator in intensive care.

By the following Monday morning, Gérard's brother, Serge (himself a physician), had arrived from France with some close friends to monitor his recovery. As messages of support flooded in for Houllier, notably from fellow managers, like Arsène Wenger, David O'Leary and Alex Ferguson, the rumour mill went into overdrive with Kenny Dalglish's name linked with a temporary return to help his old club in their hour of crisis. Liverpool were quick to issue a statement clarifying the situation: 'Gérard will definitely be out of action for several weeks and during that period Phil

Thompson will take charge of team matters while the manager recovers.'

The club and its supporters were in a state of shock. Fans trawled through internet site after internet site, flicking through Teletext, Ceefax or any other source of information just to see how the man they regarded as their saviour was doing. As McAllister's post-match interview demonstrated, the players were dazed, and unsure how they would feel about going out and performing again while their manager lay in a coma in hospital. Finally, as the team prepared to fly to the Ukraine for their next Champions League assignment, news came through that Gérard had regained consciousness and, although he remained in intensive care, his condition was stable.

A good three weeks later, as Gérard Houllier lay recuperating in hospital, he was able to grasp just how close he had come to death: 'The operation was obviously very risky. Would I wake up? How well would I be when I came round? We knew it was very serious, but not for one single moment did I feel I was going to die. The medical team are satisfied that the operation has been a total success. I owe my life to the Liverpool Cardiothoracic Centre.' The time spent in convalescence at Broadgreen gave Gérard the chance to reflect for the first time on a turbulent start to the campaign – for his team and, ominously, for him too.

For two months prior to undergoing open-heart surgery, Gérard Houllier had known that something was amiss. The new season had begun in a flurry of activity that tested Houllier's managerial skills to the limit. Before August was out, a fourth piece of silverware had been added to Liverpool's burgeoning 2001 trophy cabinet, courtesy of a 2–1 victory over Manchester United in the Charity Shield. A media commotion incited by Robbie Fowler's training ground bust-up with Phil Thompson had taken the best part of a fortnight of public bickering to resolve. Liverpool had qualified for the group stages of the Champions League. And, after a shock defeat to Bolton, Houllier had axed his goalkeeper and bought two replacements – on the same day! For Houllier, the portents throughout this chaotic sequence of events were worrying: 'August was not good for me. Nobody knew that. As manager, I did not want to show that there was something wrong. Everyone who knows me will tell you that I am a workaholic. I love my job but I was going through this spell when I was getting up and found myself reluctant to go into work which is just not me. Once I got to the training ground or Anfield I was okay, but I had to force myself.'

The outward signs that all was not as it should be first manifested themselves as Liverpool prepared for the Super Cup final against Bayern Munich in Monaco at the end of August. During the team's stay in their Monaco hotel, Gérard was surprised that, for once, he did not feel the urge to go for a swim. 'I like swimming, but I didn't feel like using the pool. Physically, I felt something was wrong, but I did not show that to my players. If you show you are weak, the team will be weak. In my mind I could not allow that to happen.' Liverpool's players duly performed to as exalted a level as Gérard could have wished for, beating the Champions League holders 3–2, after a terrific first hour, during which Michael Owen and Emile Heskey ran the Bayern defenders ragged. Liverpool had defeated arguably Europe's best team and, in doing so, presented Gérard Houllier with a remarkable fifth trophy in just six months. The benefits of their performance were not confined to Merseyside: for Houllier's adopted country an important psychological advantage had been gained for the following week, when England would lock horns with Germany in a crucial World Cup qualifying match in Munich.

Any feelings of elation within the camp, however, were quickly punctured as Liverpool went down to a defeat in only their second league match of the season at Bolton, losing to a feeble shot in the last minute of the game which Westerveld embarrassingly let slip underneath him. It was the last mistake Sander Westerveld would make as a Liverpool player. Although he had played a significant part in helping Liverpool achieve their unprecedented Treble, Houllier was now of the view that Westerveld's inconsistency was going to cost Liverpool too many points to claim the championship and therefore resolved to act decisively. He immediately dropped his Dutch goalkeeper and signed Jerzy Dudek and Chris Kirkland just before the Champions League deadline for registering new players. Westerveld could not say that he had not been warned. On the first day of pre-season training, Houllier had taken his Dutch keeper to one side, with Joe Corrigan as witness, and said: 'I'm going to sign a new goalkeeper.' When a baffled Westerveld pointed to the previous year's haul of trophies, Houllier went on: 'I said the new goalkeeper was Sander Westerveld – but he had to be better than last season, because we were in a hurry and I wanted to win the title.'

His signing of Jerzy Dudek as Westerveld's replacement was to prove inspired. In short, the Polish international's displays in his first season at Anfield went a long way to marking him out as Liverpool's best custodian since Ray Clemence. Nonetheless, recruiting Dudek *and* Kirkland at a combined cost of some £12 million in one fell swoop (albeit, in Kirkland's case, a figure largely dependent on the youngster's eventual appearance tally) did seem excessive. Houllier later justified the double signing as 'purely coincidental', although he also admitted that 'some people might find signing two goalkeepers on the same day a bit extravagant'. In fairness, Kirkland's signing – as understudy to the more experienced Dudek – was no knee-jerk reaction: Liverpool considered him an outstanding prospect and had been tracking the young Coventry keeper for 18 months. He was destined, however, for a long spell on the bench. Dudek was still only 27 and, if he performed to his potential, could conceivably keep Kirkland out of the first-team for the next few years.

As Owen, Gerrard and their team mates joined up with the England party ahead of the Munich encounter, Gérard Houllier took advantage of the international break by accompanying Rick Parry to Le Havre to sign two young French football prodigies – Antony Le Tallec and Florent Sinama Pongolle (the pair are set to arrive in time for the 2003–04 season). The trip was a success, despite intense competition for their signatures from many leading European clubs, but the heavy schedule of another day dedicated to the Liverpool cause (it was also Houllier's birthday) had taken its toll on the manager: 'I had been working on this double signing since the previous May. When I got back from France I was absolutely exhausted. Usually I would be tired the following day and then recover, but this time it took a week, which was unusual. I personally think I did too much and I made a mistake by not taking a proper holiday during the close season break. I went to the Confederation Cup in Korea to enjoy games without any involvement but I found I could not sleep.' Back in Liverpool, Gérard tried to blow the cobwebs out of his system with some intensive gym sessions but couldn't motivate himself to work as hard as he wanted. He was also having to confront the twin problems of Robbie Fowler's continued struggle to regain full fitness – and, with it, a place in Houllier's first-choice team – and the fluctuating emotions of the club's large contingent of England internationals. England's magnificent 5–1 victory over Germany was a notable triumph for Liverpool Football Club: Owen, Gerrard, Heskey, Barmby and Carragher had all been involved, and all five goals had been scored by Liverpool players (an astonishing achievement, though one overshadowed by the relentless hype surrounding David Beckham's last-minute free kick against Greece that finally cemented England's qualification for the World Cup).

In the euphoric aftermath of Munich, Houllier, while fiercely proud of their achievements, had to wrestle with the inevitable dip in form that followed such a monumental, but mentally draining, experience. For Owen and Gerrard in particular – the architects, along with Beckham, of that thrilling conquest of the Germans – the demands of media and public alike were intense: their transfer values, amidst speculation that Europe's top clubs would love to acquire either or both, soared. For Owen, with the hype of France '98 long behind him, the plaudits, like the occasional brickbats that came his way, were brushed aside nonchalantly. For the younger Steven Gerrard, it was the beginning of a difficult few weeks in which he felt constantly under pressure to perform to the level he had set himself in Munich. Gerrard's performance, while placing him at the vanguard of European football, had taken a lot out of him, more perhaps than even he realised, and the harder he worked to recapture his best form, the more his game slipped into inconsistency. The first Liverpool match after Munich was always going to prove demanding, and, somewhat inevitably, Gerrard (along with the rest of the Reds' international contingent) struggled to adjust to the cut and thrust of the Premiership. Aston Villa, their visitors, took full advantage of this collective mental lapse to record a 3–1 win. Gerrard, over-anxious to impose himself on proceedings, launched into a reckless two-footed challenge on Boateng and earned a red card, and considerable media castigation, for his troubles. Liverpool's record now read three league games played, two defeats: another underwhelming start to a Premiership campaign for Houllier to overcome.

Nonetheless, results did start to pick up, although, with the exception of a vigorous display of counter-attacking in the Merseyside derby crowned by a fine Riise goal, the performances failed to reach the heights of the previous season. Houllier was feeling increasingly worn down, even as the adrenaline rush of the new season started to kick in. Against Tottenham, Owen, who had only just come on as a substitute, pulled up with a recurrence of hamstring trouble. As Anfield emitted a collective groan at the all-too-familiar sight of Owen's fragile hamstrings giving way, the pressure was being keenly felt in the dug-out: 'When one of your key players is ruled out you want to stay focused and make the right decisions. But all I knew was that the outward look of Gérard Houllier was not what I was feeling inside – which was real exhaustion.' Gérard took himself off to France for a break, even managing to play a full 90 minutes of football with friends during his visit. But he remained unable to shake off the lethargy that had plagued him for over a month and, growing increasingly concerned, on his return to Liverpool he finally decided to see a doctor and have his blood tested. While still awaiting the results, he arranged to undergo further cardiac examinations in Paris during a stop-over on the way to Prague, where he was to meet Milan Baros, the young Czech striker on the verge of being signed by Liverpool. While obviously worried enough to arrange for two sets of tests to be conducted in quick succession, Houllier's refusal to acknowledge the danger signals and step back from his intensive workload was clearly doing him no favours. In retrospect, the crisis could have struck at any time. It was Gérard Houllier's incredibly good fortune that it happened halfway through a home match, with Anfield's medical facilities to hand, the trusted club doctor to turn to and a hospital fully equipped to deal with the emergency only a few miles away, as he himself became acutely aware in retrospect: '24 hours later we were flying to Kiev in the Ukraine for a Champions League clash. If things had gone wrong when I was in the air . . . let's just say that somebody up there must like me. I personally feel I was in the right place with the right people. It was fate.'

As it transpired, Gérard Houllier never needed to see the results of his Paris heart tests. Saturday 13 October dawned like any other big match day, Houllier looking forward to the challenge of wrestling Championship points from title rivals, Leeds: 'Before the game I was fine. I was out on the pitch talking to David O'Leary. We spoke about our families and a holiday he had enjoyed in France. Everything was all right.' By half-time, the physical meltdown that had been presaged by two months of largely ignored warning signs was in full swing and Gérard's life was about to undergo a dramatic transformation with far-reaching repercussions for him and his team.

As Houllier lay in Broadgreen Hospital, Liverpool's season was on the verge of collapse just two months in. Progress in the Champions League suddenly seemed of little consequence in comparison to the fate of the man who had guided them back into Europe's foremost competition. How long would Gérard be sidelined? Would he ever be able to return at full capacity? Could Liverpool cope in his indefinite absence? Would the players be able to maintain their concentration in training and on the pitch? These, and many other questions, occupied the club and its supporters in the immediate aftermath of the events of 13 October. The most pressing issue to resolve was who to ask to run the team in Houllier's absence.

The decision not to appoint an 'outsider' while Houllier remained indisposed seemed to the board instinctively the right one. In his three years in sole control of the club Houllier had established a stable, loyal and well-drilled back-up team that were well versed in taking his game-plan forward, from training to travel arrangements to tactics. To bring in someone else, no matter how highly thought of or connected to Liverpool – and Kenny Dalglish, for one, certainly fell into both categories – would be to invite further complications and, possibly, to endanger the very stability of Houllier's carefully developed methods. Thus it was that right-hand man, bad cop to Houllier's good cop and all-round loyal servant to the Liverpool cause, Phil Thompson, stepped into the breach. Thompson neither sought nor shunned this added responsibility. It was an honour for the former captain of Liverpool's 1981 European Cup-winning team to take charge of affairs at Anfield but, as Thompson well knew, he drank from a poisoned chalice. Unused to dealing with the insatiable hunger of the media, more at home at the training ground than the press conference, Thompson would find himself thrust into the full, unforgiving glare of the media spotlight within weeks, as he was called upon to justify the sale of Robbie Fowler to Leeds. For Thompson, the assistant manager, running the team meant a conscious redefining of his approach to dealing with the players. No longer could he berate his charges from the touchline, or bark instructions, sergeant major style, at the defence, or get involved in training ground bust-ups with star players. In short, Thompson had to tone down his act. To the surprise of many outside the club, he succeeded in doing just that, and more. His composed handling of post-match press conferences, and less animated touchline manner, together with an astute manipulation of team selection and use of substitutes, impressed the Liverpool cognoscenti.

Remarkably, after the terrible upheaval of Houllier's emergency operation, Liverpool embarked on a winning run that, by early December, saw them five points clear of their nearest rivals at the summit of the Premiership and comfortably ensconced in the second round of the Champions League. Although shocked by their manager's collapse, the players' response was to come closer together, their bond cemented by a unifying desire to 'win for Gérard'. Houllier's successful instilling of the team ethic above all else in his revolution of the club had given Liverpool the platform from which to strike back in the face of unprecedented crisis. The team's well-practised pre-match huddle took on a new, almost poignant, dimension – a public show of strength, a refusal to bow before the obstacles placed in their path.

The fight-back was immediate: a famous victory against Dynamo Kiev – the first time a British side had ever won in the Ukraine – just three days after the Leeds match. Drawing strength from adversity, Thompson marshalled his troops for a renewed onslaught on the Premiership. Successive victories at Leicester and Charlton (the former by dint of a Robbie Fowler hat trick) and a hard-fought draw in Boavista in the Champions League kept morale high within the club at a time when a couple of quick defeats could have sent the team into free-fall. Their convalescing manager took great pride in the performance of his players and staff in such trying circumstances: 'I was watching games when I was in the recovery unit. One of the team, Dr Rod Stables, said that it was very good for me to keep informed. Phil Thompson has been very good. I know that at key moments he has said to the players: "This is how Gérard Houllier would have wanted you to act or respond." I was pleased to see Michael Owen doing an interview in which he said all the players had taken note of that. Michael is only 21, but he is mature for his age. I was very encouraged when he said in his interview that the disciplines and virtues the team had learned in the game had been taught to him by the manager.'

The atmosphere that greeted the sides on the occasion of the keenly anticipated Manchester United clash – the team's first Premiership game at Anfield since the ill-fated Leeds encounter – was electric. The Kop, in a moving homage to 'Le Boss', was transformed into a mosaic of red, white and blue – a touching allusion to the French tricolore. As Houllier's name was bellowed forth time and again from the terraces, a highly charged Liverpool tore into United, Owen and Riise, with a ferocious free kick, setting the Reds on their way to a thrilling 3–1 win against their nearest rivals, a victory sealed by a towering header from the diminutive Owen. All over the pitch, the Reds were first to the ball, more committed in the tackle, more thrusting in their use of possession (tellingly, Liverpool needed only 42 per cent of that). Individual battles were won in all the key areas: Murphy's tireless work rate eclipsed Veron; Beckham, pursued relentlessly by Riise, cut a peripheral figure and was substituted long before the end; Smicer's darting runs unsettled Blanc. As news filtered through later that afternoon that Arsenal had slumped to a shock 4–2 home defeat to Charlton, it was hard to escape the sense that a discernible sea change in the Premiership hierarchy was imminent. Alex Ferguson seemed almost to acknowledge as much in his post-match summing-up: 'Liverpool had a greater hunger than us. That is a great foundation for success and that is why anyone can see that Liverpool are going to be the big threat. They are where we were four years ago.' Yet, amidst the euphoria of such a resounding victory, a nagging doubt remained about Liverpool's ability to sustain a plausible title challenge. While they may have mastered the art of stifling teams and hitting them on the counter-attack, their ability to dictate the terms of matches against inferior opponents – as surely they must – was less certain. A title-winning side needs more than one dimension to its play, no matter how expertly it is capable of executing its game-plan and a long, hard season requires a varied tactical approach from the coaching staff and the flexibility and skill to implement it by the players. Time would tell but for now, certainly, the force was with Liverpool.

However, the United performance quickly took on the impression of a high watermark in Liverpool's season as goals, if not (initially anyway) points, became harder to come by. Through November, a series of low-key, hard-working displays took the Reds to the summit of the Premiership for the first time in Houllier's reign, though in his absence. During this spell the Reds' bubble had been burst just once, by mighty Barcelona in an epic Champions League tussle at Anfield. Phil Thompson, continuing to impress in his new role as caretaker manager, was downcast after the defeat but found comfort in the words of his mentor, Gérard Houllier, who phoned to remind him to keep things in perspective: 'If someone had told you six months ago that you would beat Barcelona in the UEFA Cup semi-final and that you would go on to win another four trophies, not only qualify for the Champions League but make it through to the second round in our first attempt and be on top of the league, you wouldn't have believed them.'

Although Houllier remained sidelined, things were otherwise progressing smoothly. A disciplined 0–0 draw in Rome partly redressed the balance of the Barça reverse and meant Liverpool could look forward to renewing their Champions League adventure in the spring with an authentic chance of pushing for a quarter-final place. The team were now unbeaten in the league since the Villa World Cup hangover in early September, and three Reds' players (Gerrard, Owen and Hyypiä) had just been nominated among Europe's finest fifty by the prestigious French football journal *L'Equipe*. Then came a second bombshell in the space of a few weeks, this one self-inflicted: Robbie Fowler was on his way to fellow title challengers Leeds. The timing of the move, and Fowler's eventual destination represented, to say the least, a calculated risk on Liverpool's part. And while Phil Thompson handled the ensuing media circus calmly and in a dignified manner, the transfer did, in the short term, have the effect of taking some of the lustre off Liverpool's newly-acquired status as Premiership leaders.

The need to justify Fowler's departure was also partly responsible for Gérard Houllier making his first public announcement since his illness. Save for an emotional first return to Melwood to address his players in private in November, Houllier had not otherwise visited the club. But at the beginning of December, in a passionate speech at Liverpool's AGM, Houllier spoke, among other things, on the issue of Robbie Fowler and of his pride in the achievements of the club over the past year: 'This team is a bunch of winners. You do not win five trophies and sit on top of the league after 14 games if you are not winners and that is what we are. I came to this club with a vision. In fact, if you'll pardon the expression, I came to this club with double vision. I want this club to be the best in this country and I want this club to be the best in Europe.' Liverpool, as Gérard well knew, were still some way short of fulfilling that ambition but, as Houllier addressed his audience in the Bill Shankly Suite at Anfield, his team sat proudly on top of the Premiership, five points clear of their nearest challengers following an accomplished 2–0 victory over Middlesbrough. They were now a remarkable eleven points (with a game in hand) ahead of their nemesis, Manchester United, who were struggling in seventh place. Clearly, Liverpool had their best chance of winning the title in a decade.

Over the course of the next two months, however, the wheels threatened to come off Liverpool's trophy-laden bandwagon, as goals and victories dried up in the wake of a series of torpid, one-dimensional displays, that yielded just one win from nine Premiership matches. The sudden loss of confidence was enough to turn an, at times, methodical team into a formulaic one and expose Liverpool as, perhaps, the most inflexible of the title challengers: when the pressing, counter-attacking approach did not work, there seemed to be no radical alternative. Opposition managers had wised up to Liverpool's strategy and packed the centre of defence and midfield to squeeze the life out of Liverpool's narrow, staccato attacks. This lack of variety in approach meant that sides threatened by relegation like Southampton, Bolton and Fulham were able to come to Anfield during this period and grind out draws.

The decline, which started with a dreary goalless draw against Fulham, coincided with the in-form Hamann beginning a three-match suspension. Liverpool were to miss his stabilising influence in the crucial encounters that followed with title rivals, Chelsea and Arsenal. In fact, the 0–0 draw against Fulham may have been hugely disappointing, but was to be revealed as a veritable highlight of Liverpool's form over the coming weeks. The Reds suffered their usual spanking at Stamford Bridge, although even the most pessimistic of supporters would have struggled to envisage a 4–0 defeat (Liverpool's heaviest in ten years). The portents were not good when it was announced that Owen had not made the trip south. In the absence of Michael Owen, the team continued to lack a cutting edge – a problem that

Liverpool were busily working behind the scenes to redress. There had, inevitably, been considerable press speculation as to the identity of Fowler's replacement but none of it came close to predicting Liverpool's next foray into the transfer market.

Displaying a penchant for double signings, Liverpool followed their two-goalkeepers-in-one-day coup earlier in the season by revealing that they were ready to add not one but two strikers to their books. Again, both joined on the same day. Milan Baros' signature had been widely anticipated, as it had merely been a matter of clearing the red tape to ensure the Czech had the appropriate work permit, but the identity of Liverpool's new number nine was a shock. Out of the blue, Liverpool declared they had captured the mercurial French forward, Nicolas Anelka, on a loan deal from Paris St Germain. Houllier, typically, was still working to build Liverpool's future, even while he continued his recuperation out of the spotlight, and had played an instrumental role in persuading his former charge (from his spell as coach of the French Under-18 team) to join up with the Reds. Anelka, who had endured a wretched couple of years after falling out with Vicente Del Bosque, his boss at Real Madrid, arrived carrying before him a reputation for surliness and a monosyllabic take on dressing-room banter that made Clint Eastwood's *Man With No Name* character look like Graham Norton. However, he settled in quickly, bonding with his new team mates and evidently relishing the opportunity to stake a late claim for a place in the French World Cup squad. Not that Liverpool were risking undue damage if Anelka got up to his old tricks – they had first option to buy, but equally, could wash their hands of the deal come the summer if they wanted to. And, although he had fought to recapture his best form in recent months, Anelka was certainly a high-quality striker of proven international class – pacy, skilful, a tidy finisher. So, from all angles, the Anelka move appeared to make good sense, and amid the gloom that followed Fowler's untimely departure to Leeds, it had supporters salivating at the prospect of an Anelka–Owen combination terrorising opposition defences.

Anelka arrived just in time to watch his new team take on his old, as Arsenal visited Anfield in what was ultimately to prove the most significant encounter of the season. But Liverpool, who earlier in the season had been winning without playing to their peak, had now apparently lost the habit of grinding out results. Throughout their steady rise up the table, there had too often been an absence of fluidity and assurance in the team's passing and movement and Liverpool frequently crossed the fine line between counter-attacking and lumping the ball forward for the strikers to chase. For a club where the 'pass and move' doctrine is akin to religion, supporters found the over-reliance on long-ball tactics disconcerting. Nor did this approach fully utilise the attacking strength of Michael Owen, who would have benefited from incisive passes played on the floor. When pressed on the subject of Liverpool's defensive tactics, Thompson branded the criticism 'disgraceful' and repeated Houllier's sarcastic but well-worn '127 goals scored on the counter attack' mantra. This was all very well, but that particular refrain was starting to wear rather thin – pointing to the achievements of last season could surely not justify the performances of the current campaign. Moreover, in the Treble-winning year, cup success had bred confidence within the side and, consequently, the counter-attacking game plan had been executed with panache and verve. The current campaign was suffering from a combination of events – Houllier's illness, the disruption to players' form caused by England's increasingly tense World Cup run-in (Beckham and Scholes, it should be noted, went through a very poor patch at United), rumours of unrest among players frequently rotated from the starting line-up (Barmby, Litmanen and, of course, Fowler) and the burden of increased expectation. All of these factors played a significant role in robbing Liverpool of much of the previous season's fluency. Now, as results started to go against them, the team appeared low in self-esteem. Under duress, even the best players can forget what got them to the top of their profession, too often falling back on instinct and playing the percentage ball rather than remaining calm and confident in possession.

The Arsenal game was typical, therefore, of several Liverpool displays in the middle phase of the 2001–02 season, as the Reds were made to pay for their shortcomings by the Gunners. With the game finely balanced, the visitors were reduced to ten men after van Bronkhorst was dismissed for diving in the penalty area. Now, admittedly, playing with a man short is par for the course for Wenger's Arsenal, but for Liverpool to concede two goals at home shortly after was indefensible. More galling still was the Reds' inability to make their hour-long one-man advantage count. Passes went astray, speculative shots from outside the penalty area sailed harmlessly high and wide (Berger and Riise, in particular, seemed to be preoccupied with picking out unknown acquaintances seated in the top tier of the Kop), and the team, in general, lacked the creativity and flair necessary to break down Arsenal's resolute defence. The game ended in a disheartening 2–1 defeat.

The New Year began inauspiciously. Liverpool played out a discouraging draw with Bolton, squandering the chance to return to the top of the Premiership. Later the same day Leeds succeeded where Liverpool had failed, beating West Ham 3–0. Robbie Fowler, combining effortlessly with Smith and Viduka, scored with a glorious chip to take his tally to six goals in seven matches since his switch from Anfield. By contrast, Liverpool met Southampton twice in the space of a fortnight and took just one point from a possible six.

At St Mary's, Southampton's new stadium, Liverpool were abject, losing 2–0 with as ignominious a display as seen from the Reds in years. An early opportunity to 'lay the ghost of St Mary's', as Thompson put it, was wasted at Anfield when, after Owen had given Liverpool the lead, they again stopped playing, Gerrard limped off with a hamstring injury and Southampton duly equalised. The game ended with the players being loudly booed off the pitch, a disappointing but understandable reaction, given yet another lacklustre performance. 'The fans made their feelings known,' said Thompson. 'The crowd often tell you the way your team has played. They can be harsh – but we were extremely poor. It's not nice to hear but we can't have any complaints.' What was less forgivable was sections of the crowd cheering the announcement that Danny Murphy was to be substituted. Admittedly, Murphy was playing poorly, but he was by no means the only Red to be going through a dip in form. In fact, the midfield appeared to be suffering from a collective malaise: Smicer, Berger, McAllister and, at times, Gerrard were all struggling to impose themselves. Other players were also the butt of the supporters' frustration in this period: Bootle-born Jamie Carragher came in for some fierce criticism during the Bolton match in particular, and Heskey's lack of goals meant that he was inevitably targeted by those sections of the crowd growing more irate by the day at Fowler's prolific goalscoring run at Leeds. It was not so much the 'ghost of St Mary's' as the ghost of St Robbie which seemed to hover gloomily over Anfield. It appeared more than accidental that Liverpool's poor run of form had coincided precisely with Fowler's departure to Leeds. While Fowler may not have been contributing a great deal on the pitch, his presence in the dressing-room usually had a galvanising effect on his team mates, despite his disillusionment with the situation at Anfield immediately prior to his transfer. Fowler was Liverpool's talisman – he lifted the crowd and retained the affections of his fellow players throughout his many spats with the coaching staff. In short, the team missed him – as a person as much as for his abilities as a footballer. In both aspects, Liverpool's loss was very much Leeds' gain.

Morale was now low within the camp, with Phil Thompson becoming increasingly defensive in the face of what he saw as unjustified media criticism of his team's form. Thompson, rather disconcertingly, was also at a loss to pinpoint the reasons for the side's failings against Southampton: 'I don't know where it went wrong, it is so difficult to put your finger on a definite reason, but there weren't too many people looking for the ball out there and wanting to take control of the game. I believe that comes from a lack of self-confidence – the players are down.' While Phil Thompson was continuing to make an excellent fist of juggling the demanding roles of manager and assistant manager, it was now painfully obvious that Houllier's presence on the training ground and in the dressing-room was being sorely missed by players and coaching staff alike. Although Houllier kept in constant contact with the club, phoning Thompson four or five times a day, first from his base in Corsica, then from Paris, to offer his thoughts on team selection and to monitor the form and attitude of the players in training, he was unable to bring his personality or influence to bear. Without their figurehead and with confidence visibly draining from the team, Liverpool's title challenge appeared washed up.

For most clubs, there comes a point in the season when they have to make do with lessons rather than trophies. Liverpool were not quite there yet, but introspection was gradually superseding expectation at Anfield: defeat at Old Trafford against the new Premiership leaders would have opened up an unbridgeable gap of eight points. During Liverpool's indifferent run of form, Manchester United had surged back to their best, winning nine successive matches to make a mockery of claims by critics that they had blown their chances of a fourth consecutive title. Rather than arrive at Old Trafford with the upper hand and with United desperately seeking the points, as had seemed likely at one stage, Liverpool travelled, as always, needing to check the progress of their rivals to keep their title hopes alive. And, against the odds, they managed to do just that. After a difficult first 20 minutes, Liverpool gradually began to play with a little more freedom, stroking the ball around in midfield rather than whacking hopeful long balls toward Heskey. Gerrard, in particular, started to assert himself as United's much-vaunted midfield were out-run and out-manoeuvred. Despite playing at home, United's fear of leaving Blanc isolated against Owen's pace meant the defence were holding a line close to the edge of their own penalty area. With United defending deeper than they should have been, Liverpool began to exploit the gaps between the back four and midfield, picking off passes and slowly rediscovering the rhythm and fluency that had been missing from their play for weeks. United's tactics were to prove their undoing: with the game heading for a goalless draw, Gerrard flighted a delightful through ball into the United penalty area, and Murphy stole in to chip the ball first time into United's net, over the advancing Barthez. One–nil! United's run of victories had been broken and, in recording their second Double over the champions in successive seasons, Liverpool had reinvigorated their own waning title chances, while simultaneously boosting those of their nearest rivals, Arsenal and Leeds. For Danny Murphy, hurt by the criticism aimed at him just three days earlier, scoring the winner in front of the Stretford End for the second year running was sweet relief.

For the second successive year also, three players were sent off in an Arsenal–Liverpool fixture at Highbury. This time, the occasion was the fourth round of the FA Cup, as the Reds relinquished their grip on the trophy, losing despite playing the final 20 minutes with 10 men to Arsenal's 9. But they proved no more successful at unlocking the Gunners' depleted defence than a month earlier at Anfield. In truth, Liverpool rarely looked like scoring with Owen out of sorts and Heskey's contribution, whether playing wide right or in a more orthodox striking role, negligible. However, the match was overshadowed by the dismissal of Jamie Carragher for retaliating after being hit by a coin thrown from a spectator. He responded by foolishly hurling it back from whence it came – right under the eyes of both referee and linesman. Afterwards, Carragher was suitably contrite: 'I regret what happened at Highbury because I let the club, the fans, my team mates and myself down. I was frustrated and did it without thinking in the heat of the moment.' However, the furore caused by Carragher's response to being showered with sharp metal objects was startling. The fact that the Liverpool defender could himself have been injured and that this episode was just the latest in a series of coin-throwing incidents at football matches seemed to escape the more reactionary elements of the British press. The *Daily Mail*, in particular, took the opportunity to indulge in a typically vile attack on Carragher, calling for a Cantona-esque ban to make an example of Liverpool's young miscreant. Fortunately, commonsense prevailed and the FA handed Carragher only the mandatory three-game suspension commensurate with a sending-off for violent conduct.

Despite the cup defeat, Liverpool had put their bad spell behind them, as an eye-catching 4–0 win at Leeds emphatically proved. The build-up to the visit to Elland Road was dominated, inevitably, by media talk of Robbie Fowler exacting revenge on Houllier by firing the goals that would sound the death knell for Liverpool's championship challenge. As it was, Leeds' own title hopes were punctured after a second-half display of counter-attacking vigour reminiscent of the Reds' best football of the previous season, as Emile Heskey confirmed his return to form with two expertly poached goals. After taking seven points from a daunting run of three away matches against their nearest rivals – Manchester United, Arsenal and Leeds – Liverpool were now into their stride and with easier fixtures to follow. The title race was back on. Confidence oozed through the team as they outclassed their next opponents, Ipswich Town, with a free-flowing performance at Portman Road, running out 6–0 winners. The East Anglians were torn asunder by the speed and fluidity of Liverpool's pass-and-move football. For the fourth time in as many games, Gerrard created a goal out of nothing with an outlandish pass, exemplary in both vision and execution. Heskey was the chief beneficiary of this bout of Bergkamp-like artistry by Gerrard, taking his tally to five goals in four games. Like Leeds, Ipswich never recovered from the humiliation of having such a heavy home defeat inflicted upon them: they quickly plummeted from mid-table to the relegation zone while Leeds' slump in form ultimately cost O'Leary his job.

Liverpool had now scored ten goals in two matches: more than they had managed in the previous eleven league games put together. The reasons for such a turnaround are hard to fathom, although the confidence engendered in the camp by the victory at Old Trafford was certainly a factor. The Reds were also benefiting from Gérard Houllier's increased involvement in day-to-day affairs. Although Houllier was not yet back at Melwood, he had returned to Merseyside and was now communicating more closely with his staff and players than at any time since the onset of his illness. Key players were also hitting form at the same time, notably Gerrard and Murphy in midfield and Heskey in attack. But perhaps the most significant constituent in the side's new-found assurance was a more positive tactical approach. The Leeds and Ipswich fixtures were notable for a greater emphasis on players supporting attacks from midfield than was usually the case. Riise's switch to the left side of midfield also succeeded in adding bite and aggression to Liverpool's wide play. These various elements came together in explosive fashion for the visit of title-chasing Newcastle in early March.

For many Reds fans, the mauling of a good Newcastle side constituted the best league performance of the season. Anticipation was building inside the ground from the moment it was announced that Heskey, Owen and Anelka were set to form an attacking triumvirate of mouthwatering potential. The choice of Vladimir Smicer as one of the three midfielders confirmed that the shackles were at last being cast aside at Anfield: Liverpool were 'going for it'. (The Reds' recent goal spree had been attained on their travels – they were still struggling to break opponents down at home.) When the match finally got underway (a full hour late after floodlight failure had plunged the stadium into darkness), Liverpool quickly forced Newcastle onto the back foot. Anelka, in particular, played with a hyper-intelligent swagger, linking cleverly with his strike partners and pulling wide to tease Newcastle's bemused defenders. While the Frenchman – as a willing and effective focal point for almost all of Liverpool's attacks – was the man of the match, the ebullient Murphy was not far behind, spraying passes in all directions from his position, nominally patrolling the area around the centre-circle, although, as his first goal demonstrated, alive to the possibilities of breaking forward from deep (Murphy dashed 50 yards to meet Anelka's pull-back). This was exactly the type of performance Phil Thompson had in mind when he described Murphy as Liverpool's 'most tactically aware midfielder'.

After the Newcastle game, Gérard Houllier (who was now on the verge of returning to the front line and whose idea it had been to switch to a 4-3-3) spoke of Anelka's contribution to the team: 'Nicolas is more mature, more varied and better technically than before,' he said. 'He was a player who had to be reconstructed psychologically; now you've only got to see the number of times his team mates pass to him during a match to measure the confidence he's found and which he inspires in the team.' Lavish praise indeed, although, given Houllier's decision – made barely two months later – not to make Anelka's loan deal permanent, it is now hard to view his words in the same light.

The Nicolas Anelka episode represents one of Gérard Houllier's more intriguing moments in his time at Anfield. More obviously ruthless than his axing of the hapless Westerveld and, from a purely footballing standpoint, arguably harder to justify than the emotive sale of Fowler, Houllier's abandonment of Anelka's planned £12 million move from Paris St Germain attracted considerable criticism, some of which appears – to the outside world at least – to have been warranted. The day after the collapse of the deal had been announced in a matter-of-fact statement from the Liverpool FC press office, PSG vice-president Alain Cayzac's reaction was verging on the vituperative: 'Gérard called me. The conversation was short and cold and he told me that he did not want Nicolas any more. I told him that he was not respecting his commitments, and despite the good relationship I had with him I am very disappointed by his behaviour. Liverpool's attitude is not that of a great club.' Clearly, PSG thought that an agreement had been reached in principle, Cayzac claiming that Houllier dragged out Anelka's wage negotiations until the season was over and he no longer needed the striker. Given that Houllier first contacted PSG in March after the Newcastle game to begin finalising the move, it is hard not to have sympathy with Cayzac's view.

It is difficult to ascertain how seriously Houllier considered signing

Anelka. He certainly acted shrewdly in keeping his options open, while utilising Anelka's abilities in the push for the title. Whatever the truth, Houllier's subsequent capture of the quicksilver Senegalese forward, El Hadji Diouf, was announced only a matter of weeks after Anelka's departure and judging by the impact Diouf made on the World Cup, it is clear that Houllier (who obviously rated the player very highly) was keen to broker a deal before Diouf's transfer value soared. In other words, Houllier would have been working behind the scenes to tie up an agreement for some weeks before the tournament began at the end of May. The fact, too, that Houllier was only alerted to Diouf's availability when he heard through a contact that Valencia were poised to sign him, suggests that this may have been the reason for his apparent *volte-face* on the Anelka tranfer.

Perhaps if Liverpool had won the championship, Houllier would have felt duty-bound to keep Anelka. If so, Nicolas can blame Arsenal for that! Perhaps, too, Houllier felt that Anelka would not settle for having to play the role of regular understudy to the Owen–Heskey partnership. It was hard to know for sure how the Frenchman would react – one of the less obvious benefits of the loan deal was Anelka's ineligibility for Champions League matches (he had already represented PSG in the competition earlier in the season). Houllier could therefore pitch Anelka into the fray in the Premiership while choosing to rest either Owen or Heskey for Europe. Yet this dilemma would face Houllier whoever he brought in as the club's third striker. If it was difficult enough appeasing Litmanen and Baros (numbers four and five in the queue), it was never going to be straightforward accommodating a multi-million-pound international at or near the prime of his career. Both of Houllier's preferred targets as long-term replacement for Fowler – El Hadji Diouf (the African Footballer of the Year) and the Auxerre forward, Djbril Cissé (France's leading scorer in the 2001–02 season) – were highly coveted by Europe's leading clubs. Would Diouf or Cissé, fresh from representing their countries in the World Cup, be happy to take their place on the bench alongside the under-used Litmanen?

Of course, what went on behind closed doors will have had a significant influence on Houllier's decision not to enlist Anelka's talents for the Liverpool cause: the manager was unimpressed by the role of Anelka's infamous brothers as agents in attempting to agree a permanent deal.

Claude and Didier were banned from both Melwood and Anfield, as the negotiations (particularly regarding the agents' fees) grew heated. For his part, Anelka believed Houllier did not like him questioning team matters and he subsequently laid the blame for his departure squarely at Houllier's door: 'It seemed Gérard Houllier did not appreciate my personality. It bothers him to have someone around who could stand up to him. I had no problems with the management. It was down to the coach.' Nonetheless, he worked hard to ensure a happy outcome to negotiations, reducing his wage demands to meet Liverpool halfway. He also continued to excel on the pitch, playing his part in Liverpool's phenomenal end-of-season run (eleven wins and three draws in fifteen matches, including a run of seven straight victories). Although Anelka scored only five goals in his brief time at Anfield, his pace and intelligence livened up Liverpool's attack and he had already shown he could link well with both Owen and Heskey.

Nicolas Anelka departed Anfield distraught after Houllier finally called to inform him that he was not part of his plans. But his time at the club will be remembered warmly by the supporters. A face-saving equaliser in a derby game helps, of course, but Anelka bonded well with the Kop, who – even-handed as always – were prepared to reserve judgement on a player branded surly and disruptive during his time at Arsenal and Real Madrid. A rapport was quickly established on the back of several fine displays by Anelka and his team mates as Liverpool embarked on a run that, had it not been bettered by Arsenal's super-human efforts, would surely have brought the league title back to Anfield.

The 3–0 win over Newcastle, which represented the high watermark in Anelka's Liverpool cameo, was followed by five consecutive, mostly hard-fought victories, the most memorable of which was a last-gasp triumph over Chelsea in Gérard Houllier's first league match back at Anfield. The fillip given to the squad by Houllier's return was immense, as Sami Hyypiä acknowledged: 'We've missed his presence at Melwood and at the games because he is always positive and he can wind the team up mentally really well – especially for the big games. The boss is very good at knowing when something is not right. He'll make it right. If the team is not together, he'll notice that and bring us together.' Not even Houllier's presence on the touchline, however, could galvanise the Reds into action against Chelsea.

Liverpool had not looked like breaching the Londoners' defence (in which Gallas and Desailly were imperious) all afternoon. But, displaying a resolve and self-belief so characteristic of their returning manager's influence, Litmanen and Heskey combined in the final minute of the game to set up Vladimir Smicer for a wonderfully taken volleyed winner. The goal evoked memories of McAllister's sensational last-minute free kick against Everton 12 months previously. Briefly, the supporters wondered whether Vladi's effort would have a similar, talismanic impact. Many, too, looked to the return of Houllier as the catalyst for a winning run-in that could land the Premiership crown. It was not to be. In fact, even if Liverpool had won all their remaining fixtures they would still have finished behind Arsenal in second place. The Gunners simply refused to drop points and although Liverpool slipped up just once – in an anaemic display at Tottenham – the title race was never in their own hands.

Still, the season ended with a flourish as Liverpool recorded back-to-back home victories, scoring nine goals and, in the process, applying the coup de grace to Ipswich's vain struggle against relegation. The final Saturday of the season was a riot of colour and noise as Gary McAllister enjoyed an emotional send-off from the Kop in his last outing as a Red. The Scot was quite taken aback with the intensity of the reception he received when he made his way onto the pitch as a second-half substitute. 'That sort of ovation is usually reserved for proper Liverpool legends,' he said after taking his curtain call. 'Maybe I've made more of an impact than I'd thought.' Liverpool, too, had made significant inroads into the Arsenal–Manchester United duopoly at the high table of English football over the course of the season. For the first time since the Premiership's inception, the Reds had finished above United: an automatic place in next term's Champions League first group stage was the most tangible reward for a demanding campaign waged for so long without both Houllier and key defender Markus Babbel. Less definable and – at this stage – less clear-cut is the extent of the psychological swing in Liverpool's favour as a consequence of finally mounting an enduring and realistic title challenge into the last week of the season.

Even before the season was finished, Gérard Houllier was already paving the way for the reshaping of his team's midfield ahead of the new campaign.

Club captain Jamie Redknapp had finally reached the end of an eleven-year playing career at Anfield, one sadly wrecked by injury during Houllier's time in sole charge. It was with some reluctance that the club agreed to let Redknapp move on at the end of his contract: 'Jamie has been fantastic and pivotal in the evolution of this club,' said Houllier. 'His loyalty for Liverpool speaks for itself. He has been a great player and a great captain. He has set an example to others. I have never seen a player fight so hard to get over his setbacks. Even when he couldn't play he would encourage and cheer the lads on. My greatest memory will be of him being asked to lift the FA Cup last season.' Jamie Redknapp will not be the only departure as Houllier seeks to build on the foundation of Liverpool's most consistent season in over a decade.

WHERE NEXT FOR HOULLIER'S LIVERPOOL?

So, four years after arriving on Merseyside, confident but realistic in his expectations, how close is Gérard Houllier to fulfilling the goal he set himself of restoring Liverpool to the upper echelons of the European game? When he first addressed the task of rebuilding the club, Houllier spoke in terms of a five-year plan and warned the Reds' ever-optimistic supporters that they could not expect to see his labours bearing fruit in the short term. Houllier was right to play down the level of anticipation and was ultimately correct in his assumption that Liverpool could not be turned into Premiership champions overnight. However, 2001's memorable trophy haul, albeit trophies garnered mostly from the second tier of footballing awards – BAFTAs or Emmys, rather than Oscars – inevitably raised hopes that the 2001–02 season would bring further silverware. It did not, but the stakes have been raised once again with Liverpool's best ever Premiership finish and a points tally (80) good enough to have made them champions in four of the last seven seasons. That they were eventually pipped to pole position by a side who went unbeaten away from home throughout the entire campaign says something for the calibre of the opposition. Arsenal, playing football at as exalted a level as ever seen in England, were simply irresistible. And Liverpool succeeded in living with them (in terms of consistency, if not style) – keeping the destiny of the title race in question until the final week of the season. There was also the small matter of consigning Manchester United to their first finish outside the top two since the Premiership began, and an impressive Champions League campaign culminating in a quarter-final appearance at the first attempt. And all of this achieved with Houllier, their mentor and guiding light, incapacitated for the majority of the season.

Liverpool may not have won any trophies last term but they have now earned the right to be spoken of in the same breath as Arsenal and Manchester United. The 2001–02 season confirmed that these three sides have established a perceptible distance from their rivals. The gap that already separated Wenger and Ferguson's teams from their pursuers when Houllier first inherited the task of rebuilding Liverpool has become a gulf – in class, resources, income and stature. Houllier's Liverpool can now be considered part of an exclusive three-club elite at the zenith of British football. It is by no means inconceivable that had Gérard Houllier not assumed control of affairs at Anfield when he did, Liverpool could today be heading in the direction of Everton or Tottenham: a once-great club with a proud tradition cast in the role of also-ran. Just to have maintained their status as one of the chasing pack – a Leeds or a Newcastle – will have required Liverpool moving forward from the standards set under Evans. The first battle has been won. Houllier's Reds must now take the next step.

The next 12 months will present Gérard Houllier with a daunting challenge: for the first time since his arrival, finishing in the Champions League places will no longer constitute success. Houllier's guarded statement at the club's 2001 AGM – 'I want everyone to be aware that rapid growth is often followed by a levelling out before further progress can be achieved' – was appropriate in the context of Liverpool's trophy bonanza over the preceding six months. The club needs to be moving forward and it is testament to the winning culture bred by Houllier in his time at Anfield that anything less than the capture of a major trophy next season will be seen as failure by the club's fervent supporters. But are Liverpool now ready to take the next step and bring home the league title? The evidence is encouraging, but not conclusive.

The key lies in Houllier's ability to transform the team pattern, in a subtle and non-disruptive way, from one primarily of containment and defence to a more attacking and adventurous outlook. To reach the next level, Liverpool must learn to retain the ball better, particularly when building attacks from the back. Above all, Liverpool must switch the emphasis onto offence without sacrificing the defensive soundness that has been the basis of their resurgence under Houllier. This will require a delicate moulding of the team's approach and a high degree of technical ability to execute the more high-risk passing game, fully utilising midfield as a link between defence and attack, which is second nature to Europe's top sides. When a central defender, like Lucio or Edmilson, or a defensive midfielder like Vieira or Helguera, brings the ball out from the back, committing the opposition into making challenges in the process, space is freed for attacking midfielders and forwards to drive into. For all their undoubted qualities, the Reds' defensive lynchpins, Hyypiä and Hamann, rarely carry the ball forward in this way. Frequently, the onus is on Gerrard to make the telling pass and, at times, the pressure to do so has weighed heavily on his young shoulders.

Houllier's team also need to bring variety to their play. At times last term, they were too predictable in their approach. Just as Liverpool under Evans were heavily reliant on McManaman and Fowler for their inspiration, so the long ball delivered into space (usually by Gerrard) for Owen to run onto has become Liverpool's not-so-secret weapon under Houllier. For all his faults and inconsistencies, McManaman's ability to link the play between midfield and attack brought an added dimension to the Reds' football. Real Madrid's technical director, Jorge Valdano, on being questioned as to McManaman's usefulness to a side boasting Zidane, Raul and Figo as its creative hub, replied charmingly: 'McManaman? McManaman is connected to everybody. A football match is a game of little societies and McManaman is a member of them all.' It is telling that several of Liverpool's best displays last season featured an effective contribution by either Vladimir Smicer or Jari Litmanen – two players who, like McManaman, look to link attacks. Both are capable of raising the quality of Liverpool's passing and finding the angles necessary to prise open the best defences (think of Smicer's pass to Owen against Barcelona, for example, or Litmanen's gorgeous drag-back which won the free kick from which Heskey powered home his header against Roma).

Still, it would be wrong to suppose that Liverpool will naturally progress into an intricate, passing outfit in the mould of Real Madrid or Juventus. The model remains the all-conquering 1998–2000 era French national side and its closest equivalent in England, the high-octane counter-attacking brilliance of Wenger's Arsenal, transmuting solid defence into expansive forward play in an instant. Blistering pace and sharp interplay between the side's creative outlets are essential. As Houllier seeks the final two or three players capable of taking his team to the required level, he does so knowing that he must unearth stars capable of matching Arsenal's trio of foreign talents, Pires, Henry and Ljungberg.

Fortunately, identifying the right targets – and persuading their clubs to part with them – is a speciality of Houllier's. The signing of Senegal's El Hadji Diouf at a projected £10 million from Lens looks, if his roasting of Desailly and Leboeuf in the 2002 World Cup is anything to go by, like an excellent piece of business. Houllier is certainly excited by the prospect of unleashing him on the Premiership, describing him as someone who 'plays with his foot permanently on the gas'. He also enthuses about his possession of an important Houllier attribute – a willingness to sacrifice himself to the team ethic: 'To me, a real star is one who works for the team – rather than just hanging around the penalty area waiting for others to provide him with the ball – and that is very much the mark of Diouf. In the modern game you need that sort of player.'

Houllier has also acquired the 24-year-old Frenchman Bruno Cheyrou from Lille for the modest sum of £3.8 million. Little is known of him in England other than his reputation for possessing an explosive shot (he was Lille's leading scorer with 15 goals in the 2001–02 season). As a left-footer, he is likely to contest the left-midfield position with its present incumbents (variously, Smicer, Berger and Riise). After two injury-plagued campaigns, Patrik Berger's place in the squad appears the most under threat although Liverpool have offered the Czech a one year extension to his contract. It is to be hoped that Cheyrou makes more of an impact than his compatriot, the rarely seen Bernard Diomède, who must surely rank as Houllier's least productive signing at Liverpool (despite facing stiff competition from Meijer, Ferri and Song for that dubious accolade).

Gérard Houllier's close-season spending spree has given Liverpool ample cover in midfield, the area of the pitch felt by observers to be most in need of bolstering, given last season's occasionally toothless displays. In addition to Cheyrou, Houllier has recruited his compatriot, the 21-year-old defensive midfielder Alou Diarra, on a free transfer from Bayern Munich's reserves. Senegal's African Nations Cup captain, the combative Salif Diao is also scheduled to arrive on Merseyside from Sedan by the end of 2002. Like Diarra, Diao is primarily a deep-lying midfield player, dubbed (optimistically) the 'African Vieria'. Where this leaves the man bought with precisely this role of defensive midfield anchor in mind – Igor Biscan – is anyone's guess. Biscan may yet fulfil the immense promise of his early career, but it does not appear likely that he will do so at Liverpool. He spent much of the last campaign ploughing a lonely furrow in the reserves (although, by all accounts, acquitting himself well). However, on his rare outings in the first-team he looked short of confidence. Biscan has not yet suggested that he has the ability to impose himself on the frenetic, high-pressure environment of the Premiership.

Still, neither Diao nor Diarra are expected to feature prominently in the first eleven. The manager's base in midfield remains last term's favoured four: Gerrard, Hamann, Murphy and Smicer. Although the quartet contributed only 14 league goals between them over the course of the 2001–02 campaign, all will have an important part to play in the next phase of Houllier's revolution. In the centre, Hamann and Gerrard give the defence impressive protection, while simultaneously looking to drive the team forward. On his game Gerrard is a dynamic, thrusting presence in Liverpool's engine-room, his side's heartbeat, but too frequently of late his involvement has been curtailed by injury. After a slow start to his Anfield career, Hamann emerged during Liverpool's triumphant UEFA Cup run as a pivotal figure, especially in European games, where his patience and the high price he puts on keeping possession made him an invaluable asset. Despite a brief dip in form towards the latter stages of the 2001–02 season, Hamann outshone all comers with a starring role as Germany's defensive midfield lynchpin in his country's surprise run to the World Cup final.

The contribution of Smicer and Murphy, the other two members of Liverpool's first-choice midfield in 2001–02, has not always been as clear-cut as that of Gerrard and Hamann, at least in the eyes of a vociferous section of Liverpool's support. Smicer has also been subject to a tiresome battery of critical articles by Tommy Smith in the *Liverpool Echo*. Nevertheless, both players are valued members of Houllier's squad and brought much to the Reds' best performances in a difficult year for the team. Smicer was instrumental in the Champions League victories over Borussia Dortmund and Roma (two of the most commanding displays of the season), the Premiership victories over Manchester United and Chelsea and the ruthless exposing of Newcastle's title pretensions in March's 3–0 victory. At other times, though, he struggled to impose himself and a final goal tally of five in all competitions does not compare well with the prolific returns of Pires, Ljungberg, Beckham or Robert. By such standards must Liverpool's attacking players be judged. Similarly, Murphy's confidence – and form – oscillated throughout the term, but he was still frequently Liverpool's most creative influence, and always maintained a fearsome work rate. He fully deserved the new improved five-year deal at Anfield, and the call up (though short-lived) to Eriksson's World Cup squad which marked a happy start to his summer.

Yet, despite the qualities Gerrard, Hamann, Murphy and Smicer bring to the team, Liverpool's supporters eagerly await the arrival of a playmaker/creator in the Beckham/Pires mould. The man briefly earmarked to fill the breech was none other than Leeds' *enfant terrible* Lee Bowyer. But, after a week of protracted discussions concerning Bowyer's wage demands, Houllier, unimpressed with Bowyer's attitude, pulled the plug on his proposed £9 million move as his squad departed for their annual Swiss training camp, stating that he was 'not convinced the player had either the hunger or desire to play for the club'. It was a damning indictment of Bowyer's character. Indeed, the whole, slightly surreal, incident left a sour taste in the mouth while offering further evidence – if any was needed – of Houllier's refusal to kowtow to the money-grabbing demands of the modern footballer and his agent. Still, their manager's unwillingness to play ball with David Geiss, Bowyer's agent, was a relief for Liverpool supporters apprehensive at the prospect of publicly acclaiming a man carrying more excess baggage than a Lear jet chartered by Elton John. However, the collapse of the deal left the Reds still seeking to fill that elusive creative void in midfield.

While Liverpool continue their search for an attacking midfielder capable of providing 10–15 goals per season, in other – more settled – areas of the pitch the Reds are already a match for their nearest rivals.

Defensively, they are superior to most. In his first year in England, Jerzy Dudek has established himself as the Premiership's finest goalkeeper by some distance. If Markus Babbel can complete an inspirational comeback from the debilitating virus that sidelined him throughout almost the entire 2001–02 campaign (and the portents are encouraging, given Babbel's heavy involvement in pre-season friendlies – perhaps Chris de Burgh's crystal lamp worked after all!), then Liverpool will be able to boast a back four that is the envy of Europe (although a question mark remains as to left-back, given the uncertainty over Riise's best position). In attack, the incomparable Owen can give Liverpool an edge over any side (as Arsenal and Roma, in particular, have found to their detriment). The prospect of Houllier pairing Owen with El Hadji Diouf is one that most Liverpool supporters will be relishing. Heskey and Litmanen offer contrasting alternatives, although the difficulty of integrating Litmanen into the side is not going to go away and Heskey must improve his goals-per-game ratio if he is to retain his status as Houllier's first-choice strike partner for Owen. It will be interesting to see whether Houllier chooses to use Diouf as a wide player. At times during Senegal's memorable World Cup run, he fulfilled this role with distinction. He certainly appears to possess the versatility and fleet-of-foot to operate on the flanks. Such an approach would also enable Houllier to leave the Owen–Heskey partnership undisturbed.

The supporters believe in Houllier and trust him to make the right choices for the club. Houllier, for his part, has shown himself brave enough to make the toughest decisions – as Ince, Fowler, Ziege, Westerveld and Anelka can all testify. Similarly, players like Heskey and Murphy know that if their manager believes in them, he will keep the faith through hard times as well as good. Houllier is unwavering in his support of those who are committed to the Liverpool cause and who have shown him the desire, and ability, to succeed. It is vital that Liverpool now build on the foundations Houllier has laid – not least if the club wish to keep hold of their prize asset, Michael Owen. With a move to a new stadium imminent, the Premiership television deal with Sky soon to come up for renegotiation, the future of the transfer market far from clear and the prospect of a European superleague still refusing to evaporate, now would be as good a time as any to safeguard Liverpool's place among the elite – however it may be constituted in the years to come. The expectations of club and supporters have been whetted by Houllier's achievements thus far. Given all that he has accomplished in his time at Anfield, it may even be said that the manager (and his team) now stand on the brink of greatness. Over to you, Gérard . . .

The Stats 1998–2002

2001–02 SEASON

Final Position: 2nd
League Record: Played 38 Won 24 Drew 8 Lost 6 Points 80

Goalscorers

PLAYER	PREM	LC/SC	FA	EURO	TOTAL
Michael Owen	19	2	2	5	28
Emile Heskey	9	1		4	14
John Arne Riise	7	1			8
Danny Murphy	6			2	8
Jari Litmanen	4			3	7
Vladimir Smicer	4			1	5
Nicolas Anelka	4		1		5
Sami Hyypiä	3			2	5
Robbie Fowler	3			1	4
Steven Gerrard	3			1	4
Abel Xavier	1			1	2
Gary McAllister		2			2
Jamie Redknapp	1			1	2
Patrik Berger	1				1
Dietmar Hamann	1				1
Stephen Wright				1	1

Final Position: 3rd
League Record: Played 38 Won 20 Drew 9 Lost 9 Points 69

Goalscorers

PLAYER	PREM	LC	FA	EURO	TOTAL
Michael Owen	16	1	3	4	24
Emile Heskey	14		5	3	22
Robbie Fowler	8	6	2	1	17
Steven Gerrard	7		1	2	10
Danny Murphy	4	4	1	1	10
Nick Barmby	2	1	1	4	8
Gary McAllister	5			2	7
Vladimir Smicer	2	4	1		7
Markus Babbel	3	1	1	1	6
Sami Hyypiä	3		1		4
Patrik Berger	2				2
Dietmar Hamann	2				2
Christian Ziege	1	1			2
Jari Litmanen	1		1		2
Igor Biscan		1			1

1999–2000 SEASON

Final Position: 4th
League Record: Played 38 Won 19 Drew 10 Lost 9 Points 67

Goalscorers

PLAYER	PREM	LC	FA	EURO	TOTAL
Michael Owen	11	1			12
Titi Camara	9		1		10
Patrik Berger	9				9
Danny Murphy	3	3			6
Jamie Redknapp	3				3
David Thompson	3				3
Emile Heskey	3				3
Robbie Fowler	3				3
Sami Hyypiä	2				2
Erik Meijer		2			2
Karl-Heinz Riedle		2			2
Steven Gerrard	1				1
Vladimir Smicer	1				1
Dietmar Hamann	1				1
Dominic Matteo			1		1
Steve Staunton		1			1
Leyton Maxwell		1			1

1998–99 SEASON

Final Position: 7th
League Record: Played 38 Won 15 Drew 9 Lost 14 Points 54

Goalscorers

PLAYER	PREM	LC	FA	EURO	TOTAL
Michael Owen	18	1	2	2	23
Robbie Fowler	14	1	1	2	18
Jamie Redknapp	8			2	10
Patrik Berger	7			2	9
Paul Ince	6	1	1	1	9
Karl-Heinz Riedle	5			1	6
Steve McManaman	4			1	5
David Thompson	1				1
Jamie Carragher	1				1
Oyvind Leonhardsen	1				1
Dominic Matteo	1				1